Finding Home

Discovering the Place Where Your Soul Belongs

Colleen Johnson

Copyright ©2022 *Colleen Johnson*

All rights reserved.

Table of Contents

Dedication 3

About the Author 4

Chapter 1: Finding What a Home Is 4

Chapter 2: A Longing to Find Home 12

Chapter 3: Spiritually Homeless – Our Choices 20

Chapter 4: Emotionally Homeless – Other's Choices 30

Chapter 5: Finding Restoration 42

Chapter 6: Finding and Removing Obstacles 55

Chapter 7: Finding the With-ness of Jesus 65

Chapter 8: A Soul Open to the Mess 85

Chapter 9: A Soul at Home is Always Alert 99

Chapter 10: Where Jesus Dwells, Love Dwells 106

Chapter 11: Conclusion – Maintenance Required 115

References 131

Dedication

This book is dedicated to my husband, Doug, who helped me find what home really means. He filled it with acceptance of my quirks, made me feel like I was significant to him every day, and above all, helped me know I was safe with him and could be the woman God made me to be. I will forever be grateful that God redeemed my story by bringing Doug into it.

I also dedicate this book to two amazing people who always made me feel at home in their presence. I am sure it is because they both carried Jesus with them wherever they went. Both now reside in heaven with Him. I miss them and look forward to being at home with them someday.

First is Nathan. He was my very first nephew, and I loved to play with him as much as I could. As he grew, I could see him becoming more like Jesus. He loved so well. As a 30-year-old man with a wife and 4 small children, Nathan rescued a young man from drowning, but as he did, God brought him to his eternal home. Nathan's example of loving all the way through his life left an example of how to love like Jesus because He lives in the home of your soul.

Then there is Linda Letellier. Her life inspired this book. She always made me feel accepted, significant and safe. Her home was always a place where you were made to feel at home, but she also carried that feeling with her wherever she was. She loved Jesus, and it showed in her every essence. Linda died of liver disease, but even in death, she showed how Jesus was her home, and she was just going to finally see His face. She drew me to Jesus and to want to find my home in Jesus too.

About the Author

Colleen Johnson is a licensed Pastor with a bachelor's degree in Bible and Theology, Elementary Education and a Masters in Pastoral Counseling. She's currently on staff at Mountain Lake Alliance Church.

Married to Doug, she has three beautiful grown children, two of whom are married, and a granddaughter who she loves to hang out with and spoil.

Born in a small town, she learned the value of family, love, grace and was given a strong work ethic. She also lived in a large city for 20 years learning the importance of family and friendship. She has gone through trauma, verbal and emotional abuse, divorce, chronic pain and illness, all of which ravished her soul and carried it far from a healthy place.

Through learning how to lean into Jesus and his care, and vital soul care principles God restored and healed her and she found a safe haven for her soul to live.

Chapter 1: Finding What a Home Is

"There's no place like home"- Dorothy in Wizard of Oz

"And every house is built by someone, but God is the builder of everything" – Hebrews 3:4

It was the house of my dreams. This beautiful space that I had only seen in my mind's eye started to become a reality in 2000. From black granite countertops to a corner whirlpool bathtub in the master bedroom, each element was carefully selected to represent the picture of my desires. These five thousand square feet included twenty-foot ceilings, a wall of windows with a view of a wilderness area, and a stone fireplace in the middle of the house. I would finally have the finished laundry room and walk-in closets I had envied on each episode of HGTV's House Hunters. The unfinished basement would eventually hold a media room, complete with a large screen T.V. and stadium seating. We had even talked about adding an Endless Pool to enhance our living conditions. When I moved in during the spring of 2001, this house had everything I had ever wanted with only one problem; it was no place like home.

If you love the movie "The Wizard of Oz" as much as I do, you can clearly picture this scene in your head: Dorothy standing next to the beautiful, good witch of the north, tapping those sparkling red ruby slippers together, saying the phrase we can all quote, "There's no place like home, there's no place like home." For her, the fun adventures, colorful horses, and interesting munchkins of Oz could not hold a candle to the place she realized she belonged – that black and white, simple home with her Auntie Em. Her story reinforces the simple truth that we may not realize how much we need the true atmosphere of the home until it is gone.

Like Dorothy, I grew up in a typical farmhouse. My dad was a dairy farmer, and my mom worked with the children, and together, they created an atmosphere full of love, kindness, and peace. I was the youngest of four children, and as a family, we played games and took care of the farm animals together. My parents always encouraged us to laugh together, but there was always a level of discipline that had to be kept. So, at the young age of eight, I, like Dorothy, longed for something more. Dissatisfied with the things that seemed so unfair and cruel, I ran away to find what I thought would be better. For a short while, I chose to be homeless, lost in my own choices.

Thankfully, it didn't take a wicked witch to convince me to turn around and head for home that day. The strong wind and cold rain, sent by a loving Heavenly Father, made me realize that home was the better choice. Turning back toward the place I had left so quickly, my heels quickly tapped the gravel road as I ran toward the arms of the people who made my house a home.

The journey of my soul thus far, sadly, has reflected spiritually the choices that the young girl made back on the farm that day. I have run away from wanting a home with God, dissatisfied with the things in life that seemed unfair and cruel. I have also been drawn back to God, as my Heavenly Father's loving hand guided me through the storms of life, helping my soul find home again with him. As a result, I now look at the concept of a home differently. I believe there is a need to redefine home, how it looks and why we must find it if we are to understand why we must discover the home our soul needs. We also must understand why Jesus needs to be allowed to create your soul's environment. My purpose is to let you know how redefining the meaning of home helps us find it inside of ourselves. But first, join me in redefining the meaning of home.

What is a Home?

The dictionary defines home as "one's place of residence." [i] I hate to disagree with such an important source, but I don't think that definition adequately incorporates the true meaning of home. When I asked friends and family to give me their own definitions of home, a much clearer picture emerged – I heard it described as love, security, peace, sanctuary, acceptance, and happiness. I received words like rest, comfort, nourishment, and hope. Some gave phrases like "the place where I can be who I am and still be loved, accepted, and honored" and "the place I want to be." As I thought about it, something stood out: these were feelings, not things. No one mentioned countertops or bathtubs. No one's first thought was square footage or luxury items.

That "dream house" I described earlier did not feel like home, not because it lacked things but because it lacked the home-like feelings described above that would create the atmosphere I longed for. You see, while this house was under construction, my marriage was being demolished. The ongoing breakdown of my marriage caused the atmosphere within the house to be the antonyms of love, security, peace, sanctuary, acceptance, and happiness. My dream had become my nightmare. No matter how much heat roared from the fireplace, it did not fix the coldness permeating the air. No matter how much food my new, stainless steel, wall-mounted, double oven prepared, my soul cried for nourishment. Though I lived in that house for only three months, it could never fulfill my inner longing for home.

I believe God has put a longing for "home" in all our hearts. We have an innate desire for love, security, nourishment, and comfort; home encapsulates all these feelings. You see this reflected in every aspect of our culture. Restaurants use the phrase "homemade" to sell food. They understand that nourishment received from food "made at home" is usually better. The same is true of many hotels, which will advertise how much "like home" your stay will be, knowing we may agree to pay more just to get that feeling. Hospitals may be the only place that purposely won't give you a sense of home. They don't want us to stay too long! If you have ever stayed a few nights at a hospital, you know that home always seems like a much better place to heal.

In the last years of his life, my dad suffered from Parkinson's disease and dementia. He was able to stay in his home for quite a while, thanks to the constant care of his faithful wife. However, there came a day when that house was not the safest place for him, and he was moved from the hospital into a nursing home. Though the staff did an excellent job of caring for him and gave him the best substitute home they could, every time I went to visit him, I would hear him say, "I just want to go home." Even his dementia did not stop his ache for the place where he felt best. As Maya Angelou once said, "The ache for home lives in all of us, the safe place where we can go as we are and not be questioned."[ii] I know my dad would have completely agreed with her.

I, too, ache for a place I can simply be me, the person God made me to be, and, in that place, be accepted, significant, and secure, for hope would abound. I know from personal experience that a loving environment can do that, and the opposite environment can prevent hope. My experience during my first marriage and the building of my "dream house" taught me that a house and all its belongings do not always equal the atmosphere a home should provide.

People Affect the Environment of Home

So, what makes a house feel like home? Every show on HGTV would make you believe that the right location, color, chair, picture, or napkin will create the perfect home environment. Maybe another wall of shiplap or a new bed will give you the loving atmosphere you long for? There are plenty of ads that will try to convince you if you just order another product, your home will become the happiest place on earth. I have fallen for it time and again, but at the end of the day, it is not what's in the house that matters most, but who. You can have a beautiful house designed by HGTV's Joanna Gaines herself, but if the wrong person enters, the feeling of home will quickly fade away. You can also have a house that is very much a fixer-upper, and with the right person, it can feel like the best place in the world. It is the people invited into that space that create (or destroy) a loving and safe atmosphere of home.

When I asked my friends and family to describe home, another common word I received was "family." I agree. It is the personalities in our families that make a house come alive or make it feel empty. The family will share our ups and downs and also create our ups and downs. They share our favorite memories and the ones we can only laugh about years later. Our family members can also create memories we want to forget. It can be our family members that help us learn to love, share, take turns, and the importance of forgiveness, or they can teach us how not to do those things. When we all live under the same roof, the people we live with will affect our understanding of home.

Thankfully, much of my home life involved a loving atmosphere as I grew up and went to college, started my career, got married, and found a place of my own. So, no matter where I lived, I was always pulled back to that farm. Even in the toughest times, when life was filled with the winds of fear and failure, I would find a way to drive the miles it took to get back to the place where my dad first taught me how to love, and my mom taught me how to serve.

Redefining Home

With all due respect to the dictionary, I would like to redefine the primary definition of home with a tweak to one word. Instead of the *place* we reside in, it is the *environment* we reside in. The environment is the overall feeling a space gives you. The right home environment will be a place that has both love and peace. It will be a setting where you feel safe and nourished and will be a haven of rest, relaxation, and healing.

So, what does this have to do with our souls? The soul is the part of us that is eternal. According to the website *Got Questions*, the soul is "the immaterial part of a human being that can respond to other people. In Greek, the word for "soul" is *psyche*, from which we get the word *psychology*. The soul involves the mind and emotions. It gives us the capacity to relate to others and form bonds. It is our souls that respond to beauty and high ideals. People with healthy souls are capable of forming meaningful relationships, and people with unhealthy souls find it more difficult."[iii] Therefore, I think we all would have the goal of having a healthy soul.

Jesus was the one who emphasized that the soul was of utmost importance. In Mark 8:37 (NLT), Jesus asks a rhetorical question, and the answer is obviously "no." He said, "Is anything worth more than your soul?" If Jesus thinks our souls are worth more than anything, then making sure they are healthy should be a top priority. If any place needs to have the feeling of home, it is our soul. Thankfully, Jesus sent his Holy Spirit to reside in our souls when we invited Jesus to be our

Savior and Lord. As we stay connected to Jesus through the Holy Spirit, the atmosphere of our souls will begin to be filled with acceptance, significance, and the security of home.

However, this world we live in is full of sin, and the enemy of our souls, Satan, will do all he can to disconnect our souls from Jesus. Lies about our identity, sinful choices, family struggles, unforgiveness, wounded hearts, and fear quickly put walls that keep our souls from feeling at home. When that happens, we become desperate to get home again, like my eight-year-old self on the gravel road I ran away on. The good news is that being desperate to find a home is the first step on the journey back to Jesus and a soul filled with the atmosphere we long for.

Chapter 2: A Longing to Find Home

"Home is the nicest word there is." – Laura Ingalls Wilder

"And if I go and prepare a place for you, I will come again and will take you to myself, that where I am you may also be." – John 14:3

The size worried me. How could I adjust to only two bedrooms when I had been so used to four or more? The rooms were quaint, and the essence of a cabin was drawing me towards it. This house I could choose was, in my opinion, so much less than the last two houses I had lived in. Less square footage, smaller yard, no fireplace, and none of the character I longed for in my HGTV dreams. Yet, there was still something that made me say yes to moving here. It was the fact that I would be living with a man who really loved me. My second chance to experience a great marriage. He loved this house, so I could love it. This place would be ours with no links to my past. I knew that once we settled in, it would be the place I would find the essence of home I was desperate for.

Home: The Longing of Our Soul

When we change the definition of home from a place to an environment, though it is a minor adjustment, it creates desperation in your soul to have the atmosphere of home. As identity, acceptance, and security develop there, it will provide what you need to walk in faith, hope, and love, creating an atmosphere that replicates "Christ in me, the hope of glory."[iv]

How do we make the atmosphere of our soul feel like home? I want to take you to what I believe is the best place to find out, the Word of God. In Luke 22, we get a glimpse into the life of the disciple Peter, a person who I see as having the atmosphere of home in his soul. Yes, this is the Peter who denied Jesus three times before the crucifixion [v] but later was dramatically changed when he, along with the 120 others, received the Holy Spirit within them during Pentecost.[vi] The presence of the Spirit of Jesus in his soul made a huge impact on how he lived. He went from someone affecting the people around him with doubt[vii] to inspiring faith in them. In fact, Acts 3:41 says, "Those who believed what Peter said were baptized and added to the church that day-about 3000 in all." This only happens when the Spirit of Jesus is creating an atmosphere of home in your soul.

Later in the book of Acts, we find another short story that demonstrates how Peter, whose soul was full of the presence of Jesus and was so spiritually healthy, was able to affect those who came close enough to be in his shadow. "As a result of the apostles' work, sick people were brought out into the streets on beds and mats so that Peter's shadow might fall across some of them as he went by."[viii] Apparently, the environment of the home that resided in the soul of Peter was so powerful it could heal people! There is only one way that the atmosphere around him could do that – he had found his soul home in the presence of Jesus.

The Soul Longs for the Presence of its Creator

Though I won't meet Peter until heaven, I have met certain people who also seem to have made the presence of Jesus their soul's home. When I would get within their "shadow" or what could be referred to as the energy of their soul, then the presence of Jesus within them gave me a definite sense of being loved, accepted, and safe, bringing hope and healing with them. They would instantly make me desperate to find my soul a home with Jesus. One such person was a woman in my church whose name was Linda. She made choices that allowed the Spirit of Jesus to affect the atmosphere of her soul so powerfully that others became desperate for a home with Jesus too. She literally made you feel at home when you were in her company. Through the ups and downs of her life, she cultivated the presence of Jesus, and her soul found its home in Him. She lived in such a way that Jesus was her priority, and loving people was the result. She loved well until Jesus took her to her forever home in heaven and said with a loud shout, "well done, good and faithful servant" Her life demonstrated the need to cultivate the presence of Jesus in our souls.

In order to cultivate the presence of Jesus in our souls, I want to answer one question. What do I mean by the presence of Jesus in our souls? Let's let the Bible answer that for us. In the Bible, we see the Spirit of Jesus – the very presence of God – shown in two distinct ways. The first is the omnipresence or the truth that God is everywhere. [ix]In his book, *God on Fire,* Fred A. Hartley III states, "It is impossible to get away from His Spirit or flee from His omnipresence. God's omnipresence benefits all people equally: Hindus, Buddhists, Muslims, Jews, secularists, and atheists, as well as Christians. You can't get any more or any less of His omnipresence, nor can you alter your proximity to it".[x] God's omnipresence is in our houses, grocery stores, banks, restaurants, bars, and churches. It is the presence of God; we are often unaware of and require nothing to be with Him.

The other form of God's presence is referred to as the manifest presence. The word manifest means "readily perceived by the senses and to make evident or certain by showing or displaying"[xi] Hartley describes it like this: "By its very definition, God's manifest presence is impossible to miss. Unlike the omnipresence, God's manifest presence is selective and highly personal." I love God's manifest presence because it brings the power of His kingdom with it.

Throughout the Bible, we read of times when God clearly showed up. From walking in the Garden of Eden[xii], speaking from a burning bush[xiii], or writing on a wall[xiv], God has ways of letting us know He is there. The manifest presence of God often comes in response to prayer and affects the transformation of those who witness it. When Jesus chose to come to earth as a baby, He was the manifest presence of God. When people saw Him, touched Him, and heard Him, they were truly experiencing God in the flesh.

When Jesus ascended into heaven after his resurrection, the physical manifestation of God that Peter and the other disciples walked with ended. But only so that we would have a better one! Jesus, Himself said, "But I tell you I am going to do what is best for you. This is why I am going away. The Holy Spirit cannot come to help you until I leave. But after I am gone, I will send the Spirit to you."[xv] The Holy Spirit, also called the Spirit of Jesus,[xvi] was made available to all who trust Jesus as Lord and Savior and would reside inside the soul of all who calls on the name of the Lord Jesus Christ to be saved.

As a nine-year-old child, I prayed and asked Jesus to save me. At that moment, God deposited in my soul, the Spirit of Jesus. In 2 Corinthians 1:22, it says, "and He has identified us as His own by placing the Holy Spirit in our souls as the first installment that guarantees everything, He has promised us." This guarantee means He is, like the omnipresence, always there to make sure we get to our eternal home.

On top of that, the Spirit of Jesus, like the manifest presence, will come on me as God empowers me to do what He is asking of me at that moment. Acts 1:8 says, "But you will receive power when the Holy Spirit comes upon you. And you will be my witnesses, telling people about me everywhere." When the Holy Spirit comes on us, it is distinctly felt and enjoyed, plus it is for the benefit of others, not just us. I like to say it this way: The Spirit of Jesus is in me, for me, and on me for others.

The Presence of Jesus: the Atmosphere of Home

To help you understand how the presence of Jesus and the feelings of home are the same, I want to go back to one of the responses a friend gave when I asked what home meant to her. She said that when she thought of home, it was, as she put it, "my slice of heaven." I am not sure if she realized how right she was! Billy Graham wrote in one of his devotionals, "What kind of place is heaven? First, heaven is home. The Bible takes the word "home" with all of its tender associations and with all of its sacred memories and tells us that heaven is home."[xvii] The Bible clearly refers to heaven as our forever home. One verse says it best. 2 Corinthians 5:8 declares that heaven is home when the Apostle Paul writes, "Yes, we are of good courage, and we would rather be away from the body and at *home with the Lord"* [emphasis mine].

Why do I think heaven is described as home? Based on John 14:3, it is because Jesus is there. Jesus said, "And if I go and prepare a place for you, I will come again and will take you to myself, that where I am you may also be." Heaven will be the place where we are physically with Jesus. It is his presence that will fill that place, and therefore, it is the reason we will feel at home there.

The great news is that we don't have to wait until we die and dwell in heaven to find that feeling of home. We can have a "slice of heaven" every time we choose to surrender to and honor the Spirit of Jesus, who dwells within our souls. As we do, Jesus' power fills us with the atmosphere of home. When we find Jesus as the home of our soul, we find that "slice of heaven" we long for.

Given that the presence of Jesus is the key to finding a home, we must learn to consistently make Jesus's presence our priority. So, if you remember what I said earlier, we can't affect the omnipresence of God, and God is the one who decides whom he will manifest Himself. What can be done to make the Presence of Jesus our soul's home? I found the answer when I learned about the fourth form of Jesus' presence. It was in a book by Dr. Rob Reimer called *River Dwellers*[xviii], where I discovered what Dr. Reimer calls "The Cultivated Presence."

Cultivating is a term I am familiar with, coming from a farming family. Cultivation is described as "the loosening and breaking of the soil."[xix] My dad and brothers spent much of the summer months with this important task. The reason the soil around the plants needs to be cultivated is to eradicate weeds and encourage growth. Both are vital to better yields come harvest time. Comparably, as I learn to cultivate the soil of my soul with the presence of Jesus, I will experience similar results.

The Bible talks about cultivation in Luke 8, where Jesus is giving the Parable of the Sower. In it, He describes the kind of "soil" we need to have in our lives to produce a "crop." Luke 8:8 says, "Still other seed fell on fertile soil. This seed grew and produced a crop that was a hundred times as much as had been planted!"[xx] As a farmer's daughter, I know that to produce fertile soil, cultivation must happen. My dad made that noticeably clear. Good soil needs both the absence of weeds – which the bible refers to as "thorns" – and the presence of nutrients that promote growth. In the parable, Jesus is comparing the soil to our souls. To grow spiritually, we need our souls to be both free of "thorns" – which the Bible describes as "the cares and riches and pleasures of this life"[xxi] – and full of the nutrients, which I believe to be the time we spend in the presence of Jesus. These things combined will produce the "harvest" he asks of us.

What is that harvest? Based on the context of the story in Luke, Jesus seems to be talking about the number of people who will put their faith and trust in Him. In other words, as we cultivate the right conditions in our spirit, it will allow God's word to not only produce faith and trust in us but also allow us to help other people do the same. Every day we encounter someone that needs something only Jesus can give. People who lack peace, feel unloved, have hurt, and are full of fear. They are missing the essential feelings of home in their lives. It is as if they have become emotionally and spiritually homeless.

I will go into more detail on the specifics of how I found my soul's home by personally cultivating the presence of Jesus in my life in a later chapter. For now, I have discovered that it is imperative to learn how to cultivate Jesus' presence so that His Spirit will have full access to my soul. When we don't, we can become all become spiritually and emotionally homeless. You see, our souls become homeless when our choices and the choices of others keep our souls from finding a home.

Chapter 3: Spiritually Homeless – Our Choices

"Your separation from God is the hardest work you will ever do"- Hafez

"It's your sins that have cut you off from God. Because of your sins, he has turned away and will not listen anymore" - Isaiah 59:2

The cost was hard, and the room was cold. As I tossed and turned, trying to get comfortable, there were sounds coming from the other side of the seven-foot divider that irritated my tired mind. The tears and angry tones from the young mother next to me, who was unable to comfort her children in that damp and lonely place, haunted me. I tried to understand and sympathize, but truthfully, I just wanted to sleep. Her frustrated tone didn't surprise me. We were in a homeless shelter, the place neither of us really wanted to be. I was there supervising a group of high schoolers who were volunteering for the week. She was truly homeless, escaping an abusive marriage. I had a safe house I could go back to. She and her two children no longer had a safe place to call home. Though our situations could not have been more different, what we did have in common was a deep longing to find home: a place of love, acceptance, and safety we both needed.

This young woman, who I will call Beth, was only one of approximately 553,000 people who are experiencing homelessness on a single night in America, [xxii]one of the most tragic realities in society today. Like so many others, she found herself in a space with truly little privacy and only enough room for the two cots she shared with her children. As I approached her the next morning to see how I could help, the shame and sadness of her circumstances covered her like a storm cloud. Beth's response of "I'm okay" sounded more like a question than an answer. It told me how much she really wanted it to be true, knowing it was not. I decided to connect her children with one of the high school students for some playtime to give me a few moments with Beth so I could hopefully be the listening ear and friend she needed that day.

As Beth's story poured from her lips, the extremes in our differences started piling up. She had been raised only by her mother since her father had abandoned them when she was three years old. The only father figures she had known were the live-in boyfriends who came and went from their house for the next fifteen years of her life. Some were kind, but most ignored or abused her. The only spiritual guidance she remembers was a great grandma who would sing "Jesus Loves Me" to her and pray at meals when they visited, which hadn't been often enough. Add this up, and Beth found herself making a choice after choice to find the love, security, and acceptance she craved in the bottom of a bottle or the arms of abusive men. Now she was here, escaping her third marriage, with the clothes on her back and her two small children.

Knowing that the best way to help someone is to find something in common. I tried with Beth, but I felt unable to adequately empathize with the hardness of her past. Our backgrounds were too diverse for me to honestly say, "me too." That is until it dawned on me that as a recently divorced woman, I also knew what it was like to be rejected, to have someone say and do things to purposely hurt me. Though my children were much older, I was walking the road of single parenting with the struggle that brings. Yes, I had made choices that led me down hard paths too. Though I was not physically homeless, we shared a homelessness of the soul.

You Don't Need to be Homeless to be Homeless

I believe it was during that stay at the homeless shelter that God began to help me understand the kind of homelessness everyone experiences. This kind does not involve the absence of a physical house at all. Instead, it happens in the environment of a person's soul. It is my belief that if our core needs are not met as we mature, we cannot fully feel at home in our inner beings. These needs were established in us by our Creator God and only in Him are they met. These needs (based on Maslow's Hierarchy of Needs)[xxiii] are

- Certainty – A sense of security, safety, and comfort in the world
- Variety – A sense of change, interest, and adventure
- Significance – A sense of uniqueness, individuality, and being special
- Love & Connection – A sense of acceptance, belonging, and support
- Growth – A desire to learn, grow and evolve
- Contribution – The desire to give to those around us.

As I look over this list, I notice some familiar words – some of the same words my friends gave me when I asked for their definition of home. Both lists include feelings of love, safety, acceptance, and belonging, which, to me, absolutely describe what a home should be filled with. Both Beth and I had found out in different yet real ways that life has a way of stripping us of those needs leaving us spiritually homeless.

In chapter two, I clarified the idea that it is the presence of Jesus that gives us the essence of home. In other words, Jesus is home, and home is Jesus. There is a particularly important passage in scripture that demonstrates this to me. In Psalms 90:1, Moses is writing after his journey with the Israelites to the Promise Land. This Psalm is in a series of psalms written as the prayers of Moses. He has led God's people out of Egypt, which they thought was their home, after 400 years of dwelling there, and into the homelessness of the wilderness to give them time to learn the lessons God desired them to learn.[xxiv] Moses states clearly in this verse that "God is our home," and he speaks as someone familiar with the homelessness the desert caused. The Israelites were trying to find home in every other place but God. Wanting to either go back to Egypt or get to the new land promised by God. In this in-between space, Moses sat down to write this prayer, one he hoped that in Israel's wanderings, and maybe our own wanderings, it would teach us that nothing else will satisfy our deep longings for love, security, and acceptance, like God can.

The Need to Find Home Again

On that early spring day, as I sat with Beth sharing about Jesus, the Holy Spirit came and revealed the truth that Jesus is her soul's home, the kind of home she was really looking for. At the same time, I began to hear His still, small voice whispering how much I needed to find my home in Him again, too. She slowly began to see how spiritually homeless she was, and so did I. As we prayed together, I saw hope rise up within her, but it was rising in me too. It was not just Beth's countenance that changed as the love of Jesus flooded through her soul. We both were beginning a journey to find home began.

I remembered the joy of my salvation as a nine-year-old as I saw it rise in Beth that day. The memory of that summer day came back, and I remembered listening to the powerful message preached at that local crusade. The Holy Spirit revealed to me again how I had realized that I was not saved just because my parents were or because I went to church and was basically good. I discovered that I needed my own relationship with Jesus. On that summer day, I made my journey down the aisle to a woman who would pray with me – like I had prayed with Beth – and the Spirit of Jesus came and took up residence within my soul. I recalled how the months after that life-changing day were exciting, full of a new revelation of the love of God, the truth of my security in that love, and the peace of being forgiven. I had so much hope. I began being fascinated instead of bored by God's Word as my dad would read it to us each morning at the breakfast table, and I developed a deep desire to read it for myself.

Yet, despite my newfound hope and love, life and all its ebbs and flows soon started filling me with doubts. These doubts led to lies I sadly believed about God and about myself. One of my first memories of this happening was just a few years after I accepted Jesus into my heart. I was about twelve years old when my parents took in a foster baby whose mom had been heavily on drugs during her pregnancy. This tiny baby, due to the choices of his mom, had to endure his own drug withdrawal for the first weeks of his life. These withdrawals caused him to scream in pain, and his body stiffened for hours at a time. During those hard days, my mother became ill, so I often had to step in to care for this baby boy. The more I spent time holding him, the more my young heart and immature mind convinced me that he was my responsibility to care for. Our bond became strong, but so did the problem that was caused.

On my thirteenth birthday, social services came to our door to bring my sweet baby boy back to his mom. My broken heart and a voice in my head convinced me that God and, therefore, Jesus must not be all He was cracked up to be if He would allow this to happen to me and that baby. How could this baby be better off with his mother (who gave him up!) and not with me?" I chose to believe that I must not be good enough for the task of caring for others, and I would need to try harder and harder to please those I cared about. I had been duped by the "father of lies" (John 8:44), Satan because if he could convince me that Jesus was not a safe dwelling place, I could trust I would keep my distance from Him. Therefore, I bought into the lie and made a choice to put some distance between Jesus and me. I chose to lead my soul down a sin-filled road away from my home with Jesus, and I became spiritually homeless. This was why I started choosing much less secure places to get my needs met.

The Good and Bad of Free Will

God chose to give all humans free will. We all get to choose; we are not robots of God. Most everything we want to blame God for is actually the result of free will. Free will is something we don't want to give up, but we really hate when others choose to cause pain. As followers of Jesus, we must realize we still have the free will to make choices. Though we have the Holy Spirit in us as a guarantee of eternal life[xxv], we still are given a choice to "trust and obey," as the old hymn states.[xxvi] We can choose to "grieve the Holy Spirit" (Ephesians 4:30). We do this by not surrendering to His will and ways. As one of my friends told me recently, "we can have the salvation part down but not the Lordship part of our walk with Jesus."

Though God has always provided an amazing atmosphere of home with all we need for life[xxvii], the fall of Adam and Eve led to the part of us that loves our own way, leaving us unsatisfied with what Jesus offers. Adam and Eve had the perfect home on this earth. They were completely loved, safe, and "felt no shame."[xxviii] They walked with the presence of God daily in their lives and were entirely nourished by Him. That is until everyday life and a fallen spiritual being brought a serious temptation into their unspoiled setting. He began convincing Eve that surrendering to what the serpent said was better than surrendering to what God said. This choice of lordship was what led to their homelessness, as they were kicked out of the Garden of Eden, achieving the goal Satan has had since he, too, became homeless by being cast to the earth for his rebellion.[xxix] His desire for his own way got him kicked out of his heavenly home. In retaliation and in his jealousy, Satan has not wanted us to find our home in God either.[xxx]

Our enemy shows up in our everyday life the way he did with Adam and Eve. He tempts us to be dissatisfied with finding our home in Jesus.[xxxi] He gets us to question the goodness of God, just as he had for Eve. These doubts, allowed to linger and not taken to God for answers, are the very things that led Eve and Adam to make a choice to trust their own way instead of God's, and soon they, like Satan, found themselves kicked out of their home, [xxxii] physically and spiritually homeless.

Finding Home for Our Soul Begins with Surrender

Like Adam and Eve, the choice of who we surrender to can leave us spiritually homeless too. We find ourselves in a place where we try to satisfy our souls with the cardboard structures that the world offers us. Though we have unlimited resources available in Jesus, we can find the temporary pleasures of this world much more appealing. Like Eve, we are led to take our focus off all that we have and place it on what we don't have. For example, Adam and Eve were given an abundance of trees that were "pleasing to the eye and good for food,"[xxxiii] revealing that it was not from a lack of God's provision that they made their choice. Instead, they focused on what they lacked by not getting to eat the fruit of that one tree. I will say that I, too, have chosen to focus on what God has taken away instead of all He has given me.

Worse yet, we can make the conscious choice to stay homeless, to live separated from the presence of Jesus in our lives with all the benefits He promises for us. I once read a story of a man who lived a homeless lifestyle by living under bridges and in homeless shelters for most of his life. Those who knew him were quite shocked when they found out, after his death, that he was actually a multi-millionaire.[xxxiv] He had at his disposal the resources to live a life full of the riches our world could offer but chose to struggle with temporary structures that held no lasting promise of security and rest.

Like this man, we, as followers of Jesus, have at our disposal the richness of the kingdom of God. Yet we often choose to settle for the meager offerings of wealth, food, clothing, and material possessions or even human relationships as the structures we use to satisfy the longing of our souls. These poor substitutes only keep us in a homeless state with no promise of the abundant life God offers if we would connect our souls with Jesus.[xxxv]

  I lived this way for many years. Instead of cultivating Jesus' presence for the love I longed for, I looked to boyfriends that only rejected me when I didn't measure up to what they were longing for. Most just call it being boy crazy; now I realize it was a dangerous way of trying to meet the deep longings in my soul. On one occasion, I remember praying for a certain young man in my youth group to find me interesting enough to ask me out. When he never turned his eye toward me and instead asked out the "competition." Instead of turning to Jesus in my pain, I chose to turn toward the one boy that did give me attention, wrong attention. The trouble with the boy I turned towards was that he was interested in me only for the fact that I was, let's just say, "more developed" than some of the other girls. I know now that dwelling in the presence of Jesus would have kept me from choosing this relationship and saved me from not just rejection but lingering shame.

  Sadly, I didn't learn my lesson, and as an alternative to letting that rejection and shame point me back to finding my soul's home in Jesus, my next relationship landed me deeper in shame as I made more very regrettable decisions to keep rejection at bay. Yet, the rejection eventually happened anyway. I have learned that living on the streets of human lust only left me more homeless than before. It wasn't until I was in my first marriage to someone with the lingering traits of those first boyfriends (and who also emotionally abused and rejected me) that I, like the prodigal son in Luke 15[xxxvi], finally came to my senses and started running home to my Father God and His son, Jesus Christ. Jesus went right to work, helping me deal with the consequences of my choices. There were also the choices of others that had to be dealt with because I was not just spiritually homeless. I was emotionally homeless.

Chapter 4: Emotionally Homeless – Other's Choices

"You aren't alive if you aren't in need." – Dr. Henry Cloud

"And my God will meet all your needs according to the riches of his glory in Christ Jesus." – Philippians 4:19

  I stepped through the door with visions of an exciting new life ahead. This small apartment was the first place I would call home since moving away from the farm. I was newly married, and my hopes of joy, love, and peace were carried in along with my furniture and newly gifted kitchenware. Yet it was not long before my vision of a happy home started blurring. Those hopes I carried in were going to have to be repaired, much like the bedroom wall, which soon held the damage of my husband's anger. I went to work to hide the damage to my soul as quickly as I slid the dresser to hide the hole in our bedroom wall. The need to fix both issues would wait for a much later date.

  The good news from the last chapter is that as we make Jesus our soul's home to heal our spiritual homelessness, we find a place where we find love, security, and acceptance. The bad news is that we still deal with the uncontrollable choices of other people that will leave us emotionally wounded. When we choose to keep those wounds hidden in the closet of our home with Jesus, it results in what I call emotional homelessness. Sadly, I hid many wounds in the closet of my soul, which kept me from receiving most of the unconditional love and healing power of the presence of the Lord Jesus Christ for many years. Whether it was fear of rejection or just hiding the thoughts and emotions that I felt were too ugly for a holy and perfect God. The result was a constant battle with unhealthy negative thought patterns that kept me isolated from the only One who completely desired to help me heal and carry my hurt and pain.[xxxvii]

How Others Can Leave Us Homeless

In the book Genesis, chapter 37, there is a story that shows how the choices of others can leave us homeless. Joseph was the favored son of Jacob and was given a beautiful coat as a gift from his father and prophetic dreams from his Heavenly Father. Both gifts had filled his brothers with jealousy leading to decisions that ultimately left Joseph far from home. As a result, the safety of his father's love was replaced by the fear of his brother's hatred. The robe of his father's acceptance was replaced by the ropes of jealous actions. Quickly, Joseph found himself in a foreign land far from the hope of his father's love. To me, this demonstrates the simple truth that we can all become homeless, emotionally homeless, by the choices of those around us.

From the moment we are conceived, we interact with other people. From parents to siblings to friends, it does not take long before the actions of those around us leave us emotionally scarred. Peter Scazzero made a statement I have seen played out in my life and the lives of many of my friends and family. He said, "Very, very few people emerge out of their families of origin emotionally whole and mature."[xxxviii] I believe this is because we are more easily wounded by family because of both proximity and relationship. No matter if we have a Christian family or not, we live with people who were born to be selfish. The Bible calls this our sinful nature. Romans 3:23 says, "For all have sinned and fall short of the glory of God." Even if we have accepted Jesus as our Savior and are forgiven, which, in a spiritual sense, makes us "dead to sin,"[xxxix] we continue to have a daily choice to surrender to that truth. When we don't, our selfishness will hurt our family members, and unless forgiveness is taught and practiced, lingering bitterness and pain will remain for years.

Perceptions Versus Intentions

I want to think that in most families, much of the wounding that happens is not intentional. However, it seems that one of the schemes of our spiritual enemy is to confuse intentions and perceptions. His "steal, kill, and destroy"[xl] strategy works because he knows what humans perceive they will believe is reality. In the language of Psychologist Jim Taylor Ph.D., "Perception acts as a lens through which we view reality. Our perceptions influence how we focus on, process, remember, interpret, understand, synthesize, decide about, and act on reality. In doing so, we tend to assume that how we perceive reality is an accurate representation of what reality truly is. But it's not. The challenge is that the lens through which we perceive is often warped in the first place by our genetic predispositions, past experiences, prior knowledge, emotions, preconceived notions, self-interest, and cognitive distortions".[xli] This means that though the intention of an action or the words of the person was not meant to harm, it can feel as bad as a kick in the shins.

Some of our views of reality are partially formed due to something we can't control. That is called birth order. In my story, the perceptions of family members' actions came through the lens of being the "baby of the family". Psychologist Dr. Kevin Leman says, "Youngest is known for feeling that "nothing I do is important, none of their accomplishments seems original. Their siblings have already learned to talk, read, and ride a bike. So, parents react with less spontaneous joy at their accomplishments and may even wonder, 'Why can't he catch on faster?'" [xlii] This seems to perfectly describe much of how I felt during my growing-up years. The lie, I believe, was that when added up, I was clearly not enough to be a worthy member of my family.

My older siblings are smart, athletic, and very personable. They left powerful shadows to follow. I felt much pressure to stay on the same path they were on, never thinking it was okay to follow my own path. You know, I thought I had to go with the flow. Our competitive society causes this sibling comparison to be a powerful force in our lives. We will search for our "feeling of worth" by trying to be better than our siblings.[xliii] Though now I know the path God designed for me is powerful and unique, back then, I felt I was lacking and inept due to my differences. I don't think we are taught early enough that our combination of personality, spiritual gifts, and passions are exactly the way God plans them to be for our purpose in life. For this reason, we can be convinced by the enemy of our souls, like I was, that there are parts of us that are never good enough. Our identity lacks value.

Comparison Keeps You Homeless

Alexander Jensen, Brigham Young University researcher, said how "natural it is for younger siblings to compare themselves to their older siblings as they'll always be at a more advanced stage in their lives."[xliv] I was an expert comparison maker. My sister was outgoing, but I tended to be shy and overwhelmed in social settings. My brothers were

33

extraordinarily successful baseball and basketball players, and I struggled to find a sport I felt confident in. My siblings seemed to get on the honor roll with ease; I struggled to get Bs and Cs. In my mind, I could not measure up. I look back now and see that many of my choices were from a soul that had a felt need to over-compensate so I could hide how inadequate I thought I was. This, sadly, led me to live what I want to call a fear-based life.

Fear Keeps You Homeless

Fear became the most potent tool the enemy of my soul used to hold me back from being all God wanted me to be. I was completely afraid of failure because it would prove to the world that I was a fraud, that I really did not belong in my incredible family. In an article called, *The Effects of Sibling Competition*, Dr. Sylvia B. Rimm says this about the baby of the family; "they become dependent on the positive feedback from older siblings and may become fearful of assuming responsibilities or initiating creative activities. The youngest child may see little likelihood of becoming as competent and successful as older siblings.[xlv] I can honestly say that to this day, I crave hearing positive feedback from my siblings. I longed to hear the words "I am proud of you" from them, which coincides with being number two on the enneagram scale. It seems that no matter how many fans I had as a young person, if my older siblings didn't seem to be one of them, I was left feeling unsuccessful. As a result of these wrong perceptions in my formative years, many of those normal child-like issues in my life led to deep emotional wounds I carried with me into adulthood.

Hurt People Hurt People

I became an expert at hiding all I believed was wrong in my life. The façade I wore was layered with half-truths and hidden pain. Lying became my entangling sin. Even when my first marriage was an inner mess, I made sure that outwardly it came off as a happy home as we celebrated Christmas with my family each year. I never confessed the brutal words that were taking my personality from me. Nor could they know the depth of the eggshells I walked on each day to keep from having more anger hurled in the direction of me and my children. The emotional abuse led to brain trauma that I deal with even today. I felt my family expected me to have the peace-filled, happy homes they portrayed. You must remember I genuinely wanted them to be proud of me. Hence, I became a master magician. Hiding what I could behind the curtain while distracting them out front in an exhausting attempt to hear their applause.

But the rabbit fell out of the hat the year it was my turn to host the family Christmas. I prepped my house and set the stage. Yet, I could not hide the angry words hurled in my direction behind closed doors when I did not perform as my husband wanted. Their potential applause turned into a quick departure. Not one of them came to my rescue or seemed to want to defend me. Their choice to leave instead filled me with shame, embarrassment, and feeling very much alone. I know now that they intended to relieve me of what they believed was the cause of the issues, their presence. I also know that they thought it was the best and most peaceful way to help as a loving family. They just did not realize that I perceived it completely differently; through the lenses of the past unhealed scars I carried.

Honest intentions to help can be twisted to feel like an intentional hurt from the viewpoint of a wounded person. Since family is so deeply connected to home, it is often our family experiences that end up leaving deep wounds that can only be healed in the presence of Jesus. If we remain emotionally homeless, the wounds of one generation move down to the next. Joseph Mattera wrote in Charisma News[xlvi], "It is an old adage that 'hurt people hurt people.' Those who have been emotionally damaged tend to inflict their hurt and pain on other people." Rob Reimer writes that "family sin patterns have an unusual pull on our souls; they are often the most stubborn sin patterns to break."[xlvii] Those sin patterns will always affect us and leave us with emotional wounds in our souls. However, a family may be the starting place, but it is not the only place the hurt and pain cycle occurs. Friendships also become a road that can lead to emotional homelessness.

Along with family relationships, friendships are a powerful influence in our lives. They are also the places that lead to some wounds that wreck us emotionally. According to Michelle Anthony, Ph.D., in an article called *When Friendship Hurts*, "Learning how to make and be a friend is one of the major developmental tasks of the elementary years. It is akin to learning to read—a fundamental skill on which later skills depend. During this time, children actively seek ways to assert their own identities and to gain importance in the eyes of others. They try to find the means to be powerful. Unfortunately, because of their developmental level, young kids often don't know how they can be more powerful without it being at the expense of another." This is something they should be taught by their parents. But as Tori Rodriguez wrote in Scientific American, "The consensus is clear: mean parents make mean kids—and the victims of mean kids. Several recent studies confirm an association between strict parenting styles and children's likelihood of both being a bully and being bullied".[xlviii] This truth played out in my life as well.

When I was in sixth grade, I became friends with the daughter of our church's newest pastor. We discovered we had many things in common, including our love for Barbie and her world of make-believe. However, it was not long before my friend's extremely strict upbringing stirred something up in her that my own personality and family experience did not: rebellion and mean behavior. As we both entered seventh grade, she started hanging out with the girls that walked on paths I was never invited on. Behaviors that my parents had warned me against started to flow out of her, and roadblocks to our relationship appeared. Soon, the wounds in her heart lashed out at mine.

It was clear one day that she was strongly urged by her new friends to end her association with me. The way she chose to do this became the stuff of counseling sessions years later. From implications made to names called, I felt afraid, betrayed, and devalued. This concurs with what psychotherapist F. Diane Barth, L.C.S.W., wrote, "When those on whom we depend for love and support betray our trust, the feeling is like a stab at the heart that leaves us feeling unsafe, diminished, and alone. And this loss makes us more vulnerable physically as well as emotionally."[xlix]

Imprisoned by Damaged Emotions

The vulnerable state I was left in emotionally imprisoned me for years. The walls I placed around my soul gave me truly little room for spiritual and emotional growth. The normal maturing process is hindered when our emotions are stuck in those wounded places. I found myself holding damaged emotions in secret places so that I could control who could affect them. That secret place does the opposite of what we hope it will and instead aids in the growth of unhappiness, frustration, bitterness, and, eventually, depression. I led a double life—a dutiful Christian on the outside but an emotional mess on the inside.

No matter how "Christian" we can look on the outside when we allow the choices of others to affect our souls, we soon become a "fixer-upper." Peter Scazzero says in his book Emotionally Healthy Spirituality that "emotional health and spiritual maturity are inseparable. It is not possible to be spiritually mature while remaining emotionally immature."[1] My relationship with Jesus and with others suffered because of the barriers I put in my life to protect my soul from the pain of betrayal and rejection, thinking it was the only way to survive. Like a homeless person puts up a plywood structure to keep out the weather yet finds it never fully keeps out the cold and wind, I was using fragile structures to prevent me from getting more pain yet found myself developing an isolated and fear-filled soul.

It is clear that we can play right into the hands of our enemy, Satan, who wants us to be in that isolated, fear-filled place, away from having our soul's home with Jesus, and instead imprisoned by so much loneliness that we will justify hurting others. From abuse to abandonment, we are left in terrible emotional pain. Fear becomes the plywood structure we live in. We can quickly make the same choices that took us away from home and, in that process, lead those close to us, like our children, away with us. The home Jesus offers our souls will seem so far away that the cycle of being hurt and hurting others becomes a shelter we are living in to deal with our own homesickness. My first marriage is still one of those hard-to-talk-about chapters in my life, yet it revealed a clear example of what I am talking about.

My first husband's own childhood pain led to a need to be in control which came out in less than loving ways. The hurts of his childhood resulted in the emotional and sexual abuse directed at me. My fear-based upbringing echoed into a walking on eggshells philosophy that crippled me from all I should have been for him. He resorted to angry, hurt-filled words when I needed encouragement. When he needed encouragement, I would nag. His history with pornography resulted in me feeling more used than loved. The numbness of my emotions just left him feeling unsatisfied. He seldom felt honored, and I rarely felt loved. This unhealthy cycle steered us to the eventual end of our marriage. Neither of us chose to fully protect our children from the fear and abuses going on, creating the potential for this cycle to repeat in their lives as well.

A cycle of being hurt and hurting others leaves us with both aching hearts and poverty of the soul. Mother Teresa is quoted as saying, "The most terrible poverty is loneliness and the feeling of being unloved."[li] Feeling unloved creates a pattern of unhealthy emotional choices in our lives. Just like physical poverty can lead to physical homelessness, poverty of the soul leads to emotional homelessness. Though our society keeps trying to end physical homelessness, I can only find one way to solve emotional homelessness. Surrendering every part of our lives to dwell intimately with Jesus. He has to become my soul's home.

The Centrality of Jesus is the Key to Finding Home.

I, along with many Christians, have tried to live the Christian life without the centrality of Jesus. We can so often forget from whom we can dwell and draw. Instead, we try to build a dwelling place of our own and come up empty and hypocritical. My dwelling place of fear, loneliness, and pretending I was okay not only wreaked havoc personally, but also made me appear like a fraud. The problem with hypocrisy is that instead of drawing people in and making them also want a home in their soul with Jesus, it repels the very people we are called to reach out to, those who need Jesus' atmosphere of home the most. When Jesus is not your main dwelling place, yet you still call yourself a Christian, it will result in the form of godliness without the much-needed power of the presence of Jesus. We can easily find our home in causes, pollical agendas, and special interests instead of letting those things flow from the heart of Jesus for people. 2 Timothy 3:3-5 describes those Christians who do not dwell with Jesus as "without love, unforgiving, slanderous, without self-control, brutal, not lovers of the good, treacherous, rash, and conceited, lovers of pleasure rather than lovers of God..." These remind me of the description of the qualities of those who are spiritually and emotionally homeless in previous chapters.

The solution is to turn around and ask God to give us the key to home by cultivating the presence of Jesus in our lives. A.W. Tozer said in one of his sermons that "There is a strain of loneliness infecting many Christians, which only the presence of God can cure."[lii] When we choose to cultivate the presence of Jesus, and He becomes the home of our soul, we learn to dwell in His will and ways. As that takes place, he will start to restore us with his love, acceptance, and the security we long for. Soon, we understand how much he loves and accepts us and gives us our identity as God's child. In his presence, we also find the healing we require. The good news is that though hurting people hurt people, healing people heal people. When we are healed and leave behind our spiritual and emotional homelessness to dwell with Jesus, he starts to deal with the brokenness within. Soon we start to flow with the love, joy, and peace that all around us desire. When our much-needed restorative work begins, we begin to heal and become one of the healed people who heal people.

Chapter 5: Finding Restoration

"The work of restoration cannot begin until a problem is fully faced." — Dan Allender

"For it is God who works in you to will and to act in order to fulfill his good purpose." – Philippians 2:13

    The door did not open quietly. Rusty hinges and age made a loud screeching as I attempted to enter the abandoned farmhouse. My friend and I had always been curious about what this run-down farm site contained. We were finally brave enough to find out. Our adolescent imaginations were quite sure it was haunted, and the story of how was just waiting to be told. The smell we encountered as we entered added to both our intrigue and fear. Behind the wall on the left was a kitchen full of the remnants of a person who had once cooked in this space used; pots, pans, a crooked fork, and a chipped glass bowl were strewn about, now unusable. On the right was an exposed bedroom now empty of its intended use. In front of us, the paint-stripped door to the attic was stuck due to a cracked foundation, but we worked together to pull it open enough to climb up and find the treasures we were sure it held. Those squeaky steps were less of a problem than the slam of the door behind us. As we swiftly rode our bikes away on that stormy summer day, we knew that my home was a much better place to be.

The Hope of Restoration

    If you could have entered my soul around the time of my divorce, it may have looked much like that abandoned farmhouse of my childhood. Behind the walls I had built around my soul, there were remnants of the gifts God had given me, but the years of abuse and neglect had left them mostly unusable. My private struggles, no longer hidden, left me feeling fully exposed to the elements of criticism and shame I felt I deserved. Worst of all, the sheer terror of the door of my dreams slamming shut behind me caused hope to flee away as far as it could.

In the middle of the devastation that life choices and subsequent consequences had caused, God continued to love me through some amazing people who showed me how Jesus could become the home of my soul. As I soon learned to cultivate the presence of Jesus in my life daily, it began to open my life's rusty door, and I began to make Jesus my dwelling place. I realized that Jesus was the true source of love, acceptance, and security. It was with Him I would find healing. I could finally hold on to the promise that Jesus would never abandon me[liii]. I will be forever thankful that Jesus didn't turn away from the scary, messy place the home of my soul had become. Instead, as Jesus started to become my dwelling place again, He initiated a process of renewal and renovation that continues to transform me back into the masterpiece He designed.

Renovation Starts with the Foundation

I must admit that I, like many others, am a huge fan of HGTV's show *Fixer Upper*. Though I have had truly little experience with renovation, I certainly love to see the process happen. I love to spend a lazy Saturday watching a "Fixer Upper" marathon. Recently, on one of the episodes, I was brought back to the image of that old house I described at the beginning of this chapter. It was season two, and episode number five, where they took an old house called the "Dutch Door House" and transformed it into an amazing place to live.[liv] I started imagining if that old farmhouse I had feared as a child had been put in the hands of Chip and Joanna Gaines instead of allowed to deteriorate, it could have made an amazing home. Both homes had similar potential and similar problems. One statement by Joanna stood out to me. She said as they walked into the bathroom, "So, it's scary in here, but from what I see, obviously, the foundation is the biggest issue. Once that's fixed, I feel it has a ton of potential." This may have been exactly what Jesus would say as I invited Him in to do something about the condition of my soul. Once the foundation of my soul was fixed, there was a lot of potential inside me.

Like that house, my biggest issue was not that I didn't have a foundation of my identity in Christ but that it was damaged by years of neglectful choices. Choices made because of misinformation, a lack of understanding, and, yes, even rebellion. My foundation was built on who Jesus Christ[lv] said I was on that summer day when I asked Him to be both my Savior and Lord. However, as described in Matthew 7, we have a choice to build our lives on the rock of believing in Jesus or the "sinking sand"[lvi] of disbelief. I was choosing the latter more often than the former by not practicing His presence and trusting in His word. As a result, my soul's foundation was cracked. That foundation had a crack in who I believed I was. I had stopped believing who Jesus says I am. My identity needed serious repair. Choosing to give Jesus an open the door to my soul would repair the cracks in the foundation of my soul.

The Foundation of Identity

Jesus started the renovation process by correcting the very foundation of my identity. According to Webster's Dictionary, identity is defined as "the distinguishing character or personality of an individual."[lvii] In other words, it is who you are at the core. In the book *Soul Care*, Dr. Rob Reimer says, "What you believe about yourself is the foundation of your life; it is your identity, and a faulty foundation will create cracks in your soul." Those "cracks" start when who you believe you are is found in the wrong places. Technically, the only person who has the right to give something its identity is the one who created it. In the case of human beings, that would be God.[lviii]

God created humans to basically crave three things; acceptance, significance, and security. He then gave those first humans exactly what they craved in a relationship with Him. However, a serpent whose identity is that of a liar came into the picture and started convincing Eve to doubt what God said. In Genesis 3:1, Satan began his sentence with four tricky words, "Did God really say…" He says the same to you and me. Did God really say you are accepted? Did God really say you are significant? And did God really say you are secure? We, like Eve, quickly decide that we must have heard God wrong. Thus, the lies become beliefs that pound cracks into the foundation of our soul's home.

Since we tend to become what we believe we are, [lix] we are tempted by Satan to believe lies. In a transformational book called *Lies Women Believe*, Nancy DeMoss says, "Deception was – and still is – crucial to Satan's strategy. According to Jesus, it is the devil's very nature to deceive:

'[The devil] was a murderer from the beginning, not holding to the truth, for there is no truth in him. When he lies, he speaks his native language, for he is a liar and the father of lies.'[lx] He is also called an "Angel of Light"[lxi] to let us know that these lies are so disguised to look truthful we are quite easily swayed in this fallen world. I think I can safely say that you will not meet a woman who has not struggled with believing a lie about who she is. The enemy knows the danger a woman (and a man) can be to his mission of destruction if they really live the truth of who God says that she is.

Because of the danger to the enemy's plan that anyone who is living out the truth of who they are in Christ, there are three specific lies that the Angel of Light gets us to take hold of. Rob Reimer describes these as the performance lie, the people-pleasing lie, and the control lie.[lxii] When Jesus died on the cross, He declared that everyone was worth dying for. Our worth was settled on that day, and it has not changed. However, when we don't believe this, we can try to find our value in other places.

The performance lie says that we only have value if we perform how others expect us to perform. The truth, on the other hand, is that you will never live up to everyone's expectations. Jesus' death on the cross declared your performance null and void. Performance is no longer linked to the value He puts on you. You are still worth dying for, no matter how you perform. Do your best, but don't let the lie that your performance will ever make you more or less valuable. You are always valuable in the eyes of Jesus, and He is the only one that counts.

The people-pleasing lie says that you only have worth if people like you. Guess what? Other people do not get to decide on your value. They can like you or not, but that does not change the fact that you are worth dying for. You hold value because "Jesus loves you, this I know." Plus, He can never stop loving you. Romans 8:39 declares that "Neither height nor depth, nor anything else in all creation, will be able to separate us from the love of God that is in Christ Jesus our Lord." The truth is that you can't please everyone. I have learned this the hard way as a seasoned people-pleaser. The truth is that your value is never in having people like you or how many likes you get on Facebook or Instagram but is always in the fact that Jesus says you are valuable no matter what.

The lie of control is that your value depends on if you are in control. The problem is that control is elusive, but we all want it. Dr. Reimer reminds us that when we try to control others, they will feel "manipulated, shamed, judged, condemned, and bullied."[lxiii] I know this to be true from living with a control freak for 16 years. He only thought he was okay if he could control everything and everyone around him, which included me and his children. I wish he could have seen the lie in that thinking. The truth is that he was valuable no matter how much control he had. The truth is that there are things we can control and a whole lot of things we can't. Either way, our value was settled at the cross of Jesus Christ, who gave up his control to come to earth and die for our sins because we were worth dying for.

Jesus wanted to remedy the destruction of those lies in my life by refurbishing His original design. Messages and books came into my path that reminded me of who God says I am as His child. From chosen[lxiv] to a saint[lxv] and from a joint heir[lxvi] to a friend of Jesus[lxvii], each one fills my spirit with truth and joy. I chose to review them often, especially when my thoughts and feelings were declaring the opposite. Here is a brief list from Neil Anderson's *Who I am in Christ*[lxviii]

Accepted in Christ: I am accepted (Romans 15:17), God's child (John 1:12-13), Christ's friend (John 15: 12-17), been justified (Romans 5:1), belong to God (1 Corinthians 6:19-20), a saint (Ephesians 1:1), have direct access to God through the Holy Spirit (Ephesians 2:17-18), redeemed and forgiven (Colossians 1:13-14), and complete (Colossians 2:9-10).

Secure in Christ: I am secure (Proverbs 3:19-26), free from condemnation (Romans 8:1-2), cannot be separated from Christ's love (Romans 8:35-39), established, anointed, sealed by God (2 Corinthians 1:21-22), hidden in Christ (Colossians 3:3), a citizen of heaven (Philippians 3:20), have a spirit of power, love and a sound mind (2 Timothy 1:7), can find grace and mercy (Hebrew 4:16), and I am born of God so the evil one cannot touch me (1 John 5:18-20).

Significant in Christ: I am significant (1 Corinthian 3:9; 4: 1-2), salt and light of the world (Matthew 5:13-16), have been chosen and appointed to bear spiritual fruit (John 15:16-17), personal witness for Christ (Acts 1:8), minister of reconciliation (2 Corinthians 5:17-20), God's workmanship (Ephesians 2:10), can approach God with freedom and confidence (Ephesians 3:12), and can do all things in Christ's strength (Philippians 4: 11-13).

In John 8:32, the writer tells us that "Then you will know the truth, and the truth will set you free." However, this is one of those times in Scripture when we find an if/then promise. In the verse right before we read, "Jesus said, "If you *hold to* my teaching, you are really my disciples" (John 8:31, emphasis mine). The only way we will find the freedom that truth gives is to hold on to that truth like a carpenter holds on to a hammer. Every time the enemy or the world tries to try to get me to loosen my grip on the truth with a lie about who I am, I grip tighter to pound in the truth statements of who I am in Christ. Choose to renounce the lie and announce the truth of God out loud if you can. It will defeat the enemy every time you proclaim it in the name of Jesus Christ. Try saying this each time:

"In the name of Jesus Christ my Lord I renounce the lie that (fill in the lie you are tempted to believe), And I announce the truth that (fill in the identity in Christ statement). From this day forward, I choose to believe all that Father God says about me in Christ."

The Foundation of Forgiveness

Once I fully started to hold on to the truth of who I am in Christ, Jesus started to deal with another crack in my foundation. The crack of unforgiveness. This began as I started to sense Him at night in my dreams. I remember getting very vivid dreams that involved specific people I had a difficult history with. I guess it felt a little like the story of Ebenezer Scrooge being brought back to the past to see what he hadn't realized at the time and needed to grasp now. These dreams, once processed, gave me new perspectives on these people, resulting in a change in what I believed about the importance of forgiveness. It became obvious that the first principles I needed to adjust were the ones I believed about other people. As I started to see these people from a new viewpoint, the view that hurt people hurt people, I found that God needed to fix the crack in my foundation caused by unforgiveness.

For most of my life, I did not understand the power of unforgiveness and how foundational forgiveness is. According to Rob Reimer, "Harboring unforgiveness is like putting up a welcome sign in our souls for the enemy to come in and wreak havoc, and he never rejects an invitation."[lxix] In other words, I had not only invited Jesus in, but I was also inviting the enemy to take up residence in my life through unforgiveness. Before any more could be done in the home of my soul, Jesus needed to kick out the other resident I had let in. You see, Jesus and the enemy cannot be roommates. Forgiveness is like the eviction notice that kicks the opponent out.

The first step was for Jesus to fix my viewpoint of forgiveness. I had always viewed myself as a forgiving person. When I was offended or hurt by someone, I would push it away or even end up blaming myself because dealing with that person's actions brought possible conflict, fear of rejection, or at the very least, made that person unhappy with me. I realize now how unhealthy that form of reconciliation was. I am not sure what word a psychologist would use to describe my reactions to being offended or hurt, but I know it would not have defined true forgiveness.

Psychologists will define forgiveness as a "conscious, deliberate decision to release feelings of resentment or vengeance toward a person or group who has harmed you, regardless of whether they actually deserve your forgiveness."[lxx] That was not what I was doing. I had not been releasing anyone; I had been both keeping them captive and keeping myself a prisoner. This problem became clear as I studied Isaiah 61. In this section, we find a prophetic passage telling us what Christ will do when he comes and is quoted by Him in Luke 4 as He begins His ministry. In both places, we find these words, "He has sent me to bind up the brokenhearted, to proclaim freedom for the captives and release from darkness for the prisoners." Do you see the clear distinction between a captive and a prisoner was given there? Why was this distinction made? Though the definitions are similar, the difference comes in how someone gets there.

Let me explain it this way; you would be a captive because of the choices of someone else, but you would be a prisoner by your own actions. For instance, if a child is kidnapped, they are held captive. The child did nothing to cause this captivity and, therefore, simply needs to be rescued. Now, when the kidnapper is caught and prosecuted, he becomes a prisoner. This person broke the law and is being punished for their behavior. He needs to serve his time and be released or given a pardon to get out free. What you and I need to understand is that it works this way with forgiveness too.

What God's word means when it says that Jesus will "proclaim freedom for the captives" is that by dying on the cross in the act of forgiving us, he rescued us from being captive by the power of sin. Jesus is our redeemer! By the very act of accepting this freedom as we choose Jesus as our Lord and Savior, we are no longer held by the "kidnapper" called death. (See Romans 6:23) However, even though we are no longer captive to sin and death, we can still become a prisoner by our own choices: choices to sin and choices not to forgive.

Notice the phrasing of the next part of Isaiah 61:1, "release from darkness for the prisoners." It is in Matthew 18 where we find the best description of what it means to be a prisoner of unforgiveness. In this parable, told by Jesus, we meet a servant who both needed forgiveness and to forgive. The King forgave freely, just like Jesus, the King of kings does, but the servant did not follow suit. His choice of unforgiveness got him imprisoned with tormentors until he paid back what he owed. Later in Matthew 18:35, Jesus states, "This is how my Heavenly Father will treat each of you unless you forgive your brother from your heart."

I don't know about you, but I thought it should be the person who hurt me that would be handed over to tormentors, not me. It appears that is not how it works in the Kingdom of God. The truth is that unforgiveness leaves us tormented. When I recognized that by burying my pain and hurt instead of working through the process of forgiveness, I was tormented by the hostile spiritual forces who were darkening my mental health, which would torment my physical and emotional health as well.

Mayo Clinic did a study that found that "if you're unforgiving, you might: bring anger and bitterness into every relationship and new experience, become depressed or anxious, and feel that your life lacks meaning or purpose, or that you're at odds with your spiritual beliefs." [lxxi] I was experiencing all of these without realizing that it was the torment of unforgiveness. I was trying to fix all these symptoms with doctors, medicines, and even Bible Study and prayer for years when the only cure would be to follow the imperative command of Jesus, the Great Physician, to forgive.

Compassion Renovates Unforgiveness

Those God-given dreams first revealed my need to forgive my ex-husband. These visions started showing me, in unforgettable imagery, the hurts and wounds in his soul, and I started to really understand the meaning of the phrase "hurt people hurt people." Then one day, as I was sorting through one of my boxes left over from my move, I came across a real-life picture of my ex-husband as a child. His father was posing with his twin boys, brandishing a copy of Playboy magazine. I closed my eyes at the heart-breaking sight, yet at the same moment received one of the greatest tools God gave me in the process of forgiveness. He flooded me with compassion. Jesus helped me see this man through His loving eyes. Compassion confirmed my need to forgive. Then God showed me something even more powerful that nailed forgiveness into my soul.

Repentance Renovates Unforgiveness

It was another dream that instigated full forgiveness. This dream did not even have my ex-husband in it. Instead, there was a mirror showing my reflection, including my own hurtful choices. I saw that my thought life had made me just as much of an adulterer, a truth Jesus explained in Matthew 5:28. My reflection revealed that I am a liar, a hypocrite, and a sinner. The pride reflecting back at me was as brutal as the pride I would call out in my ex. The person in the mirror needed forgiveness as much as he did. I woke up that morning with tears of humility and a heart aching to let go of any right to keep captive this man I had married and been rejected by. I quickly reached for words I learned in a recent inner healing seminar. "I choose to forgive ____for____ causing me to feel_____I will not make them pay for the emotional pain and consequences that they have caused me. I ask You, Lord Jesus, to take back the ground I gave to the enemy through my unforgiveness, and I yield that ground back to your control."[lxxii] I then put my name into that equation.

Such freedom flooded my soul, but this was only the beginning. I continued and did the same for my siblings, my parents, my friends, and even the people who had inflicted harm on my ex. Over the next months, as God revealed person after person that needed my forgiveness, I would follow these steps. I learned the reason; I believe Jesus tells us to forgive "seventy times seven times" in Matthew 18:22. Forgiveness is an ongoing process. Just last week, I experienced another of the consequences of divorce and was reminded to forgive again. We must all understand the importance of being freed from the prison of unforgiveness and freeing those we are keeping captive by it. To help me with this, I keep a copy of this prayer of forgiveness close to my favorite chair so that when the Holy Spirit reveals someone I need to forgive, I can go quickly through the process again.

Now that my foundations were restored, it was time to remove some barriers keeping me away from the connection with Jesus that would make my soul clear for him to enter every part of my soul.

Chapter 6: Finding and Removing Obstacles

"Across Europe, this wall will fall. For it cannot withstand faith; it cannot withstand truth". – Ronald Reagan

"By faith the walls of Jericho fell, after the army had marched around them for seven days" – Hebrews 11:30

There was something out of the ordinary. I had never been in a house that was so noticeably walled off. I mean, every room was separated, and you could only enter through a lockable door. This both fascinated me and made me feel uncomfortable. I was about to spend ten days with a family in Romania while I was on a mission trip with my church. I asked my host family about the unique design of their home, and they explained that since the country had been under communist rule until 1989, when the Romanian leader Nicolai Ceausescu was removed, there was much fear of being spied upon. These walls and doors kept conversations safe and people protected. Though that need no longer existed for them, they had not yet made any attempt to open the space. These fearful people still lived with a deep need for protection, and these walls and doors were still the places they found them.

Walls of Self-Protection Must Come Down

Protection and feeling safe is one of our primary needs. In Maslow's hierarchy of needs,[lxxiii] safety is the second most important need that humans have. Because of this, Maslow says, in his scientific language, "We may then fairly describe the whole organism as a safety-seeking mechanism."[lxxiv] In my words, we all do what we can to keep ourselves safe. From having a guard dog to carrying a gun, we will do what we can to feel protected. In our homes, we erect walls, put locks on doors, and install security systems in hopes of having a safe zone for us and our families.

One of the main elements I heard when I did that survey of my friends about the meaning of home is that it should be a "place we feel safe." I am sure you would agree in this crime-ridden world we live in. There are important reasons to keep some people out and have control over who we let in. Every time we listen to or read the news, we find another reason to make our environment more secure. Wisdom says we should do what we can, yet I have also heard of extreme examples of people desperately seeking protection. The words "fortress" and "bunker" come to mind. Like in the story of the family of Bruce Burns, who starred in the National Geographic Channel's *Doomsday Castle,* which premiered on August 13, 2013?[lxxv] The article about them penned, "To prepare for the inevitable, he and his family have built a fortified castle atop a large foothill deep in the woods of South Carolina, complete with a drawbridge, portcullis, and an underground bunker."[lxxvi] It was clear that you could go too far in an attempt to protect yourself.

It also appears that those who go to these extreme measures have had experiences in their lives to make them believe that normal safety measures are not enough to keep them protected. These untrusting people have lost their belief in those who are supposed to be doing the protecting and have taken matters into their own hands. You see, when it comes to protection, trust is a very key element. If trust is broken, our sense of safety will be affected, and since we all have that "safety-seeking mechanism," we will erect our own ways to get the security we need both physically and emotionally. Just as physical structures are built to protect our bodies, walls of self-protection are created to keep our emotions safe.

Trusting Jesus Breaks Down Walls of Broken Trust

Trust, or should I say the breaking of trust, is the main reason we build emotional walls. Trust is defined as a "firm belief in the reliability, truth, ability, or strength of someone or something." [lxxvii] We build this belief in everyday interactions with others and through life situations. As Brene Brown puts it in her talk, *The Anatomy of Trust*, "Trust is like a jar of marbles. When someone does something trustworthy, they get a marble, and when they do something untrustworthy, they get one taken out." She also mentions that trust is built in the small moments of life. Those moments when you or someone you know shows up on time or keeps a promise made, trust happens. Mistrust, on the other hand, happens when your friend is late or breaks a promise they made. Every situation builds something, either the opening of trust or a wall of self-protection.

Continually broken trust will naturally cause us to put up a barrier of protection from the associated pain it causes, both the physical and emotional pain that we need to prevent from happening again. Emotional barricades seem like the most effective way of protecting ourselves but will end up closing us off from real love and fellowship with others and, yes, even with Jesus. That was my experience.

I spent most of my life living behind a wall of self-protection. As you read through chapter two, you heard of a few situations in my life that added brick upon brick to that wall because I felt I could not trust members of my family and a few of my friends. Every hurt put another brick in that wall. Mortared by unforgiveness and painted with shame, it did a good job of keeping others out, including those who could help, like Jesus Himself. I shared less and less of my heart when I was hurting. I tried to limit my need for people. In fear, I tried to control my outer façade to reflect what I believed others wanted me to be. I learned how to regulate the image they saw. All the while, behind that wall of self-protection was lurking the darkness of self-hatred and loneliness. As ministry leader Tom Zawacki says, "Beware; the same walls erected to protect our hearts can also imprison them."

The thing is, we don't need to build these walls at all. God has put structures in place to protect us. He tells us that He is our hiding place (Psalm 32:7). Nevertheless, we can choose not to trust Him and take matters into our own hands. God's walls are his promises and the instructions on how to follow His will and His ways that were designed to work in this world God created. He has told us how to live, pray, serve, and worship. He gave us pictures of His faithfulness so we can depend on Him, but God also gave us a choice on which walls we keep or which we tear down. With the fallen nature comes a problem. Our tendency is, as Wendy Speaks writes, "we do what we want and follow our own passions. Brick by brick, we choose which walls stay up and which walls come down."[lxxviii] Like the foolish woman in Proverbs who tore the good walls down "with her own hands,"[lxxix] my choices, my lack of trust in God, and my fear made me get rid of many of the good structures and become imprisoned by ones of my own choosing.

In these prisons, these walls of our own choosing obstruct our view just as the physical ones do. I realize now that the walls of self-protection prevented me from having a proper perspective on many situations. And remember what I said earlier, your perspective becomes your reality. Without a proper perspective, you are blinded to the only thing that can heal you, the love of Jesus and His protection. When you don't feel His love, His safe presence, you put in place poor strongholds that keep you from being fully who you were meant to be and the plans God has for your life. I found, however, that when I let Jesus tear down those walls and rebuild His[lxxx], I found the freedom and wholeness God meant me to have all along. The more of Jesus' presence I let into my life, the clearer it became that some walls of self-protection needed to stay down. I also realized that the only way it could was to let Jesus remove the wall of fear I was trapped behind.

Fear is an Another Wall that Must Come Down

Fear had been with me for as long as I can remember. I am not sure where it started, but I know that it was the enemy's weapon meant to steal, kill, and destroy me. As Dietrich Bonhoeffer puts it, "Fear is, somehow or other, the archenemy itself. It crouches in people's hearts. It hollows out their insides until their resistance and strength are spent, and they suddenly break down. Fear secretly gnaws and eats at all the ties that bind a person to God and to others, and when in a time of need that person reaches for those ties and clings to them, they break, and the individual sinks back into himself or herself, helpless and despairing, while hell rejoices." [lxxxi]

Hell rejoiced every time I chose to close a door to people and opportunities because of fear. The rejoicing continued as I pushed Jesus farther out the door while grieving each disappointment of a situation I thought He could have fixed. I worked overtime to control how people saw me. I somehow convinced myself that I could even fool Jesus. Nevertheless, I learned that no matter how hard I tried, I was not the regulator of people's reactions and was not in control of how Jesus wanted my path to look. I thought locking myself behind the door of fear was a safe place to be. I discovered that it was instead a dark, lonely, depressing place to be.

Jesus needed me to see that what can feel safe can actually be the most dangerous place to be. We are not meant to be locked behind any door. His Spirit's whole desire is for us to be free. 2 Corinthians 3:17 clearly says, "Now the Lord is the Spirit, and where the Spirit of the Lord is, there is freedom." Freedom from fear, fear of rejection, fear of being out of control, fear of being seen, scars, and all. The remedy to fear is faith. We have the ability to choose faith even when it doesn't feel like it. Rob Reimer writes that "we can feel afraid and act on faith, but we can't act on both."[lxxxii] King David, in the book of Psalms, knew that fear must be attended to. He gave us an example of how to deal with it when he wrote, "Search me, O God, and know my heart; *test me and know my anxious thoughts*" (Psalm 139:23-24, emphasis mine). Allowing the presence of Jesus to test your every anxious thought is the tool that takes down fear.

Truth is Our Sledgehammer

As I make Jesus my home, my dwelling place, He has used a tool that sets us all free, God's truth.[lxxxiii] I have since found that this truth Jesus speaks has a power I had never realized before. Though truth has been defined in many ways, especially in our world today, I have learned that the only source with healing power is the truth defined by Jesus. This definition is found in the intercessory prayer of Jesus in John 17. Jesus prays for His disciples, "Sanctify them in the truth: [God's] word is truth."[lxxxiv] So, what God says is true, is truth, and anything opposed to that is a lie. I have come to clearly see that, as Cindy Bultema[lxxxv] states, "Jesus saved my life, but His truth saved my mind."

    I feel that Jesus led me on a clear path to find this truth as I crossed paths with a sweet young woman named Nancy. She was involved in a ministry called SOZO[lxxxvi]. Sozo is the Greek word in the Bible that has been translated as either saved, healed, or delivered. This salvation, healing, and deliverance are the kinds that show up in our day-to-day lives, in the middle of the messes we are in. Sozo is a present-tense saving. A way Christ will give us wholeness of the healing of the body, mind, and soul in the now. According to Andy Reese, president of the Freedom Resource, "Sozo is a God-led framework helping to free individuals from the effects of wounding and sin and delivering people from the snares and presence of the demonic. It is done in overt partnership with God through finding past and present believed lies and points of access and removing or changing them, establishing healing, blessing, and obedience in their proper place, restoring individuals to a relationship with Papa God and a more fruitful and fulfilling walk."[lxxxvii]

    As I met with Nancy in our SOZO session, I grasped that this was not going to be like other counseling I had experienced. Our time together was all about moment-by-moment dependence on the Holy Spirit showing up and "leading us into all truth."[lxxxviii] As we prayed, Nancy first invited the Holy Spirit to come and be both our protector from any enemy spirits and the counselor we would need. She then showed me how to ask Jesus questions and wait on a response. That day, I learned the incredible secret of Jeremiah 33:3, which says, "*Ask me, and I will tell you* remarkable secrets you do not know…" [Emphasis mine]

Nancy soon led me to ask the question, "What is the lie I believe about you, Jesus?" As I quietly waited, I saw a clear word in my mind's eye, "untrustworthy." I knew it was Holy Spirit led the moment I heard it. There had been many times that I felt Jesus had not shown up and changed a situation the way I thought He should. I equated trustworthiness with fixing what I wanted to be fixed. How could I trust someone who had the power to stop something but had clearly chosen not to? Whether that was the death of my nephew or the divorce I had to endure, Jesus had not come through how I thought He would or should, so I had unknowingly marked Him as untrustworthy.

Now I was faced with the fact that, though I professed Jesus as my Savior and Lord, I had lived as if I could not trust Him to be either. An inner battle commenced as I went to the next step in the SOZO session, which was to ask the next question, "What is the truth?" I expected to simply hear the word trustworthy, but instead, I heard the phrase "what I say, I will do" in my heart. Though I have the knowledge that God is faithful to do what He has promised, my heart was not fully accepting it. You see, I want Him to do what I say or even what I think He has said instead of the agenda of His will, and when that does not take place, disappointment and mistrust fill my heart. Jesus was asking me to let go of my itinerary, my wants, and my ways of thinking things should be and focus first on His word and look for His ways from His perspective. The knowledge of the trustworthy nature of Jesus took a journey that day from my thoughts to my soul, where He wanted to dwell.

The great thing about this Sozo kind of saving, healing, and delivering is that it is a daily and ongoing process. By the end of that session, I had a specific tool to daily take down the wall of fear and keep it down every time I felt the need to put a brick back up. This wonderful and effective tool is the act of declaring God's name out loud over my situation. Yes, it is declaring in prayer who He is that helps me overcome the fear of who I am not. As I declare who He is, I surrender to God's character, and I can sense His grace covering all my imperfections and failings. Knowing His character starts a flow of His unconditional, sacrificial love for me and mine. This quote by Dietrich Bonhoeffer says it all.

"But the human being doesn't have to be afraid; we should not be afraid! That is what makes us different from all other creatures. In the midst of every situation where there is no way out, where nothing is clear, where it is our fault, we know that there is hope, and this hope is called: Thy will be done, yes, Thy will is being done. 'This world must fall. God stands above all, his thoughts unswayed, his Word unstayed, his will forever our ground and hope.' Do you ask: How do you know? Then we name the name of the One who does the evil inside us recoil, which makes fear and anxiety themselves tremble with fear and puts them to flight. We name the One who overcame fear and led it captive in the victory procession, who has nailed it to the cross and committed it to oblivion; we name the One who is the shout of victory of humankind redeemed from the fear of death – Jesus Christ, the Crucified and Living One. He alone is Lord over fear; it knows him as its master; it gives way to him alone. So, look to Christ when you are afraid, think of Christ, keep him before your eyes, call upon Christ and pray to him, believe that he is with you now, helping you…Then fear will grow pale and fade away, and you will be free through your faith in our strong and living Savior, Jesus" Christ."[lxxxix]

Finally, Free to be Yourself

Without the walls of self-protection and fear, we are free to be who we were made to be, to live out our call through every assignment of this life. God's restoration brings much-needed maturity. I am more determined than ever to never build those walls again and make sure that all I have is surrender to Jesus. As a result, I hope to have many more opportunities to bring the victory I have received to those God sends in my path. I have found that when we let hurting people see the scars that result from a life lived in a broken world, we connect in a common space. This open space is a place we all can feel safe to be ourselves. This is only found in the withness of Jesus

Chapter 7: Finding the With-ness of Jesus

"Be with someone who will take care of you. Not materialistically, but take care of your soul, your well-being, your heart." – Anonymous

"On the evening of that first day of the week, when the disciples were together, with the doors locked for fear of the Jewish leaders, Jesus came and stood among them and said, 'Peace be with you!'" —John 20:19

  How in the world could something so small hold so much responsibility? The weight of the keys I was handed felt much heavier than they should. I was the owner of a house; yes, just me. The awe I felt as I took in the view of this beautiful house held both fear and amazement; an all-brick exterior with vines winding up and down the outside like it was in the English countryside. Contained within were five bedrooms, hardwood floors, and two gas fireplaces. I wanted to pinch myself as I viewed this dream house I could call mine. At the same time, I wanted to snap myself out of the nightmare that had become my life. Holding these keys further verified the fact that in this house, there would be no co-owner, no man by my side. I was a single mom in charge of three teenagers and the head of this dwelling, all alone. Loneliness was keeping this house from finding the atmosphere of home.

  That loneliness, however, led to one of the best decisions I made in creating my own home. It was to make what I will call an open-door policy. You see, I needed "with-ness," and I knew others did too. I grew up with a maternal grandmother who had a "no need to knock" policy for her grandchildren. She lived a block from my school, and I could come and go and bring any of my friends over whenever I wanted, no questions asked. Her cookies and zwieback (German rolls) were always fresh and abundant and freely handed out as we came into her small 1950s kitchen. My Grandma Jensen just wanted to be with us. I now desired that same welcoming atmosphere in my home. When my children's friends needed a place to be, my house was theirs. I felt it was important that they feel that I loved to be *with* them and they were always welcome.

The With-ness of Jesus

Jesus reveals in the Bible how much He loves to be with us. From "I am with you always, even to the end of the age"[xc] to "never will I leave you; never will I forsake you,"[xci] we are assured of the power of, what I will call, the "with-ness" of Jesus. In the language of Skye Jethani, "God's focus and desire have been to be **with** his people. He walked in the garden with the man and the woman and sought to rule over creation **with** them. And the crescendo of history in Revelation celebrated the reunion of God and humanity...Fulfilling God's desire to be with us is why Jesus went to the cross... It is only when we grasp God's unyielding desire to be with us that we begin to see the ultimate purpose of the cross. It is more than a vehicle to rescue us from death; it transports us into the arms of Life."[xcii]

What Jesus accomplished on the cross takes away the need to live the Christian life alone. The important thing we need to understand is that though He strongly desires to be with us and no walls or locked doors will keep Him out,[xciii] He is not rude or demanding. He gives us a choice, yes that free will thing to invite His presence in. In fact, in Revelation 20:5,

Jesus says, here I am! I stand at the door and knock. If anyone hears my voice and **opens the door**, I will come in and eat **with** that person, and they **with** me." [Emphasis mine] Many have referred to this verse when speaking of the invitation to salvation, but if you look at the context, Jesus is speaking to the church; yes, Christians. It reveals that you can be a Christian and keep Jesus behind the door of your soul. A scary thought, yet I did it for years. Jesus, knowing that in our humanness, we will try to walk the spiritual life without Him, continually reminds us to invite Him in every day. To keep an open-door policy *with* Him.

We should always have an open-door policy for Jesus. I remember hearing this clearly as I read the following during a module of the College of Prayer International, "Christ stands at the front door of your life and knocks. He wants you to open the door and welcome Him in. It does not matter how much junk is on the floor or how much garbage needs to be removed. Christ wants you to just open the door and welcome His manifest presence. If you give Him space, He will do the rest."[xciv] It goes on further to explain some of the amazing things God does as you take this step of trust and obedience. Jesus Christ comes in and forgives and starts to heal your emotional wounds. He tears down the walls of self-protection and the lies that Satan has established as strongholds and generational issues. Best of all, Jesus comes in and brings the love, joy, hope, and peace you are longing for.

Did you notice who does all those things? It is Jesus! Our part is the act of surrender to invite Him in. We must choose to live *with* Jesus daily, sometimes minute by minute, by giving him free access to our every emotion. Back in chapter two, I introduced the idea that cultivating the presence of Jesus is the key to an atmosphere of home in your soul. The first step is making Jesus the place where you dwell. He must be fully in your soul's home before you can be all you were meant to be when His presence develops an atmosphere of home in us. The power of this comes when we can eventually carry that atmosphere to those in our sphere of influence. That starts to change the world.

My journey to cultivate the presence of Jesus and make my soul His home has been long and continues to develop, but it is something I chose to practice every day. As a former volleyball coach, I know the importance of practice. I had an ongoing rule that if you don't practice, you don't play. Those who wanted to be a better player did the most work at practice, and it was those girls who showed the biggest improvement. The practice it takes to cultivate the presence of Jesus works the same way.

Ann Voskamp, in her book *One Thousand Gifts,* says, "Practice is the hardest part of learning, and training is the essence of transformation."[xcv] I had told my volleyball girls at the beginning of the season to expect to want to quit every once and a while. I say the same to you. There will be moments and days when it will feel like it is too hard to practice keeping your soul a place for Jesus to dwell. I feel it at least once a week. You will be convinced that going back to your normal religious activity is easier. Don't give up! Its worth is immeasurable when you see the eventual transformation in yourself and in those you will influence for Jesus.

As a woman in my late 50s, I know that my physical body fights me whenever I try to get it into shape, and sadly my spiritual self isn't' any different. Have you heard the saying, "Life is what happens to us while we are making other plans?"[xcvi] Well, it is true! I have found that just a few weeks or even days into developing important practices, I get hit by a series of hard days, either with my illness or a situational crisis. On top of that, I can't emphasize enough that it is our enemy's plan to keep us away from finding our soul's home in Jesus. Making habits that cultivate the presence of Jesus in our lives will be a battle. Expect it, anticipate it, and prepare for it. However, I can most assuredly tell you that it is one worth fighting. As a follower of Jesus, we have been given all the weapons we need. Jesus wants us to win that battle and has given us spiritual weapons to fight with[xcvii]. Just check out Ephesians 5 for more on that. For now, I want to encourage you to start practicing cultivating the presence of Jesus in your everyday walk.

To help you, here are some of the practices I am working into my life, and I believe to be God-given ways to keep an open-door policy for Jesus in your soul.

Surrender is the Entry Way:

I was taught early in life that when I entered someone's home, I was to be respectful with an emphasis on asking for things politely, listening, and obeying. I needed to learn who was in charge when we visited a person's home. The same was true when people visited us; they were to be respectful of our property and belongings. People who come into your home are under your authority. The rule was that when you entered someone else's home, you surrendered your right to do what you wanted. Permission is asked for and respected.

Conversely, I have learned that this rule does not apply when it comes to inviting Jesus into your life. In fact, the rule is reversed. We give Jesus respectful authority over our home. I equate asking Jesus into our souls with asking a world ruler to come over. I think if I chose to ask Queen Elisabeth into my home, I would still ask her if I could use the bathroom. I understand that her authority would not change just by entering my home. Jesus, as King of kings and Lord of Lords, is always our authority. When we make the decision to dwell with Him, to make Him at home in our soul, we must surrender our right to do what we want. We need to ask permission and respect His authority for Jesus to truly be welcomed to stay.

As the song goes, "all to Jesus, I surrender; all to Him I freely give."[xcviii] But you and I know that is easier said than done. Depending on your temperament, the word surrender can get a different response, but I think everyone has a tough time with the idea of surrendering. Surrender must be combined with trust to be a healthy decision. When we know the person we are surrendering has our best interest in mind, it becomes much easier to do.

The more you read and study who Jesus is in the Gospels, the more surrender to Him seems like the best choice. In the resource portion of this book, I have listed all the names of Jesus from A to Z, and I have resorted to that list on many occasions when I have felt the need to surrender my will and ways to who He is. The fact that Jesus suffered and died for me should be enough to tell me He is trustworthy, but there is much more evidence in His word and in my journey with Him to choose to surrender daily.

Three areas where I consistently practice surrendering to Jesus.

1. I must surrender my will. Just as Jesus prayed in the garden of Gethsemane, "yet not my will, but yours be done,"[xcix] he asks us to do the same.

2. I must surrender my time. To quote Andrew Murray, "If you are not willing to sacrifice time to get alone with him, and to give him time every day to work in you, and to keep up the link of connection between you and himself, he cannot give you that blessing of His unbroken fellowship."[c]

3. I must surrender my soul. "Being filled with the Spirit is simply this - having my whole nature yielded to His power. When the whole soul is yielded to the Holy Spirit, God Himself will fill it."[ci]

When I have chosen to stop practicing surrender, my life gets harder. Like what happened to those girls on my volleyball team that missed practice and were unable to get as much playing time when the game came because it affected their ability to help the team. Without practice, you can't improve. I agree with A. W. Tozer, when he said, "The reason many are still troubled, still seeking, still making little forward progress, is because they haven't yet come to the end of themselves. We're still trying to give orders and interfering with God's work within us."[cii] The opposite is also true. When I release my worries, my desire for control, and my own ways and let God's work happen, I find I feel the love, peace, joy, and rest of being at home.

Prayer is the Living Room

I love the definition the Free Dictionary gives of what we call the Living Room of our home. It is "a room where people can sit and talk and relax."[ciii] In the Living Room of my home, I have expressed who I am with the way I have decorated it because I can be myself there. I have made that room, above all others, the most comfortable place to invite people into. My living room is the place relationship is built and expressed. Literally, it is a room full of life. This is why I equate the living room of our soul with prayer.

The hymn "I Surrender All" lyrics includes the following. "I will ever love and trust Him, In His presence daily live." It is this daily living in His presence that I call prayer. You see, it was in this process of making Jesus my soul's home that God taught me to rearrange and redefine prayer. Prayer became about developing my relationship with Him before all else. No prayer lists or personal agendas. This new idea of prayer was quite the switch from the prayer meetings I attended growing up. Though I was correctly taught that prayer was about communication with God, it had left out the idea that prayer was more importantly about being with Jesus.

In the language of Skye Jethani, "Coming to see prayer as communion and not just communication changes its place in the Christian life. If God is truly our treasure, and if we have faith that through Christ, we have been united with him, then prayer ceases to be a Christian's duty and becomes our joy because it is how we experience our treasure in the now."[civ] The more I came to realize that Jesus is the treasure I seek, the home I need, the less prayer was about getting Him on my side and instead about getting on His. As Lysa TerKeurst puts it, "when I pray, I position my heart to see and receive what God is already doing. I just need to stop trying to fix, control, and achieve. What God wants me to do is to slow down enough to receive what he has for me. He has the answer. He is the solution. And I can rest in these truths."[cv] Now, as I pray with this in mind, the times I spend in prayer are the times I feel my soul is most at home.

How does this look in my life? Communion with Jesus begins as I open my eyes in the morning. I talk to Him long before I get out of bed. I find that the best way to start a day is to surrender my thoughts to the presence of Jesus. The most transformational book I read on prayer is called *Everything by Prayer*: Armin Gesswein's Keys to Spirit-Filled Living by Fred A Hartley III. Armin had a very unique view of the Lord's Prayer in the Bible. He called it "The Lord's Prayer pattern."[cvi]

In this pattern, he teaches us to start with our relationship. He says in Jesus teaching His disciples and us, in Luke 11:1-4, to start with "Our Father," "Christ is making it clear that we are not praying for a relationship but from a relationship. We don't pray so that God will love us more; He already loves us as much as He ever will. He wants us to start each day and each prayer with a conscious awareness of His love and blessing toward us".[cvii] The following is the Lord's Prayer Pattern from the first module of the College of Prayer, International.[cviii]

The Lord's prayer pattern is the most foundational prayer ever given. There are 7 key parts to the model Jesus gives us:

1. Relationship – "Our Father in heaven," All true prayer begins by receiving God's love and recognizing the relationship you have with Father God through Christ.

2. Worship – "Hallowed be your name," All true prayer responds to the revelation of the glory of God's Name. It is appropriate to declare the value of His Name, emphasizing the names of God particular to your situation.

3. Lordship – "Your kingdom come; your will be done on earth as it is in heaven." Once you declare the glory of His Name, you call for the advancement of His Kingdom's reign. Praying the Kingdom includes praying for the Holy Spirit.

4. Sonship – "Give us today our daily bread. Forgive us our debts." There are two basic needs a child has: food and forgiveness. Your God brings in the groceries (food), and He takes out the garbage (forgiveness).

5. Fellowship – "As we forgive our debtors." With the forgiveness you have received from Christ, you are able to extend forgiveness to others.

6. Leadership – "Lead us not into temptation but deliver us from the evil one." Your two greatest enemies are sin and Satan. This portion of the Lord's prayer pattern confronts both these enemies.

7. Ownership – "For yours is the Kingdom and the power and the glory forever." * All true prayer moves towards Christ's ownership over all things. *While it is likely the words were not originally included in the Bible, they were probably used by Jesus, so they were included in later texts.*

Believe me, using this pattern while being aware of the love of Jesus is where I must start. Often my first uttered words each day are a simple "I need you, Jesus," followed by a quiet time of waiting to sense His loving presence before I begin.

On the days I am battling the most, from exhaustion or pain, I find I will need to take a deep breath, followed by putting my right hand on the tattoo I have that is a cross with flowers and the name Jesus on top and the word Enough on the bottom. This reminds me to be thankful that Jesus is always enough for my life, and I am always enough with Jesus with me. I will pray that I understand that, because I am His, I carry the enough-ness of Jesus, and at that moment, He never fails to fill me with His love and peace. Missionary Heidi Baker says, "Run the race. Learn how to lean into Jesus. Let Him hold you close until you can hear the rhythm of His heartbeat. Then you will know when to rest, when to run, and when to release."

The more I have practiced this technique, the more I am quickly led to worship. This worship most often comes in the way of music for me, though it can also be in other ways, like reminding me who I am talking to by recalling some of the many names of God. I love to listen to the music that leads me to long for and honor Jesus, so I fill my house, car, and office with worship. Because of this, I am not surprised when I have lyrics from a worship song playing in my brain upon waking in the morning. I know this is one of God's ways of both showing me His love and leading me in a direction for the day.

In addition, I desire to surrender and be led by Jesus through His Holy Spirit; I have developed the practice of listening to Him more than speaking to Him. Someone once told me to pray to God's face, not just His hands. It's about getting to hear from Him, not about always getting something from Him. It was a few years into my move back to my hometown that God started teaching me how to hear His voice. I found a verse that has turned out to be one of my life verses.

It is Jeremiah 33:3, where God says, "Ask of me, and I will tell you great and mighty things you do not know." Dr. Rob Reiner tells us about "Theology 101: God is smart, and He knows stuff we don't know. And sometimes, He likes to tell us what He knows."[cix] Building a relationship requires two-way communication, and the Bible teaches that as one of His children, I should be able to discern what He is saying.[cx] Yet, this had been another part of the Bible I was never taught about. When I decided to find my soul's home in Jesus, He started, let's just say, home-schooling me.

Like the best teacher, the Holy Spirit teaches each of us uniquely as one who knows our personality and gifts so well: He did create us, after all. For me, the first lessons came in dreams I did not understand but knew I needed to. Soon after, I started a study of the book of Daniel, which gave me some revelation into dream interpretation; how God uses dreams to speak to His people. Next, I felt that God led me to gifted people who helped me understand my God-given gift to understand the images He was showing me in my night visions. Psalm 16:7 says, "I will bless the LORD who has given me counsel; my heart also instructs me in the night seasons." In this training season, I began experiencing the fulfillment of many of the dreams I was given. I learned quickly that having Jesus as my dwelling place is full of the adventure of seeing God's hand at work.

Now, as a part of my prayer time, I often ask the question, "What am I supposed to do with what you just showed me? The wonderful part is He has answered that question in very unique ways. I have had the answer come as a verse of scripture in the reading plan for that day or through a song playing on the radio as I get into my car to head to work.

I have also had an instant impression of the answer, but most often, it comes as I continue to lean into his presence throughout the day, week, or month. Some answers have taken years, and some have not happened yet, so I just keep asking like it says in Mathew 7:7 "Keep on asking, and you will receive what you ask for. Keep on seeking, and you will find. Keep on knocking, and the door will be opened to you." God has always been faithful to answer in His timing.

God also speaks to me through other means. I am a visual person, so He often gives me images of pictures or words that come to my mind that will lead to the wisdom I can give, and I quickly realize that I am not its source. Why? Because I learn from the very thing, I am saying. The more time I spend in His cultivated presence, my senses become tuned into what God is doing, and I can respond in prayer and actions that work in His plan, not mine. Rarely has God spoken audibly, but I do clearly remember a time when I was driving to a conference, and as I was approaching a traffic light about to turn red. As I slowed, I audibly heard the words "move over" three times in a row. Though I hesitated at first, I made my way into the left lane before I stopped. I soon realized why it had been necessary. By doing so, I avoided being hit by a car behind me that was not going to stop at the light. The point is that listening to God amid life makes a difference, sometimes a life-or-death difference, which has added wonderful adventures to my life with Jesus.

Just like the Living Room is the place I bring those who visit my home into, prayer is the place I bring the needs of people also. The more I saw God's willingness to talk to me, the more I let Him lead the intercessory part of my prayer practices. I went from just praying from my prayer lists to finding out His list for me with the question, "who needs more of you today, Jesus?" Sometimes His list is shorter than mine, but then again, it has also been longer. Names flood into my consciousness. Most of the time, I know why. Other times, I don't. Either way, I pray what God puts on my heart to pray. I figure He knows better than I do what will work in their situation. I try to stay in a place of surrender where it is "not my will, but yours be done,"[cxi] especially when it comes to praying for my children and family.

I have found that this is the only way I can pray, or I can quickly get discouraged by what my eyes witness each day. God's goodness does not always look how I think it should look, but I am learning to trust His ways because I have seen them work out better than mine. When I again ask how I should pray for the person God puts on my heart, I will often be led to a passage of scripture. Praying God's word is the best way to see answers to your prayers because you are literally praying God's words back to Him.

I must add that there are days that most of what I have written above is too hard. Whether it is from my physical health or my mental health, I can find myself in a very desperate place. It is then that I go back to a practice I learned from an Orthodox friend of mine. She called it the Jesus Prayer. I was told to simply pray, "Lord Jesus Christ, Son of God, have mercy on me." I use it as a humble cry for help on those times and days when I don't have anything left and don't know where to start. As I repeat it, His presence comes, sometimes as a calm assurance or just the peace in knowing who He is, the one who saves and who is in charge. Anthony Bloom says, "The Jesus Prayer, more than any other," helps us to be able to "stand in God's presence." This means that the

Jesus Prayer helps us to focus our mind exclusively on God with "no other thought" occupying our mind but the thought of God. At this moment, when our mind is totally concentrated on God, we discover a very personal and direct relationship with Him".[cxii]

It is the acknowledgment of who God is that truly makes a difference in my prayers. Like the Jesus Prayer, using the names of God as both a declaration and cry for help has been my lifeline during the most difficult moments of my life. When I can declare that He is Jehovah Jireh, my provider, I find myself breathing a sigh of relief when I don't know how my need will be met. Every time I have practiced proclaiming this name, I have seen Him faithful. All in all, the living room of prayer is a great place for our souls to hang out.

Reading God's Word is the Fireplace.

One of my favorite elements of the house I shared at the beginning of this chapter was that it had a fireplace in the living room. This came in very handy during the cold winters of Minnesota. I was also thankful that it was a gas fireplace that I could flip on with a switch. Within seconds I could feel the heat flow around my body and take the chill out of the air affected so often by the below-zero temperatures outside. It was that roaring fire that kept me in that room. It was the glow of the heat radiating toward me that made leaving that room hard. Those long winter months made that living room and fireplace together a necessary part of every day.

Therefore, I parallel God's Word to a fireplace. There is an article by Charles Spurgeon where he stated, "When asked, 'what is more important: Prayer or Reading the Bible?' I ask, 'what is more important: Breathing in or Breathing out?'" It is in the combination of prayer and Bible study that we breathe life into our relationship with the living God. I passionately believe that the best way to understand and interpret the Bible is out of that kind of relationship with God through faith in Jesus Christ. "I must be with Jesus daily to fully know what God is saying in His word, remembering that one of the names of Jesus is "The Word of God."[cxiii] God's Word is the necessary fire that keeps our souls sustainable in Jesus. They cannot be separated without dangerous effects.

I spent many times over the years reading the Bible out of habit or simply out to check it off my to-do list. It was what Christians do, right? I have read the Bible through in a year many times over, but now I wonder how much of that time I was spending in the presence of Jesus. I agree with Dr. Reimer, who said, "The purpose of reading the bible is not to get to know the bible. The purpose of reading your bible is to get to know God".[cxiv]

When I simply studied the Bible to know the Bible, without the guidance of the Holy Spirit, who is the presence of Jesus in us, I mistakenly used scripture to justify myself and to hurt others through judgment and shame. I know many have done the same to me. Without the counseling and convicting power of the presence of Jesus while we read and study the Bible, we can put expectations on ourselves and others that were never meant to be carried. I am learning that knowing the Word of God and knowing the God of the Word must go together. If it doesn't, the Bible has and can become a tool of the enemy.

This was never more evident to me when, on a two-week mission trip to Romania, I met a man who knew the

Bible better than me and well enough to use it like Satan did when he tempted Christ.[cxv] He could pull scripture out of context to suit his every argument. On one of the days of our trip, as we were singing and praising God on the streets of the city, I was approached by this young gentleman carrying a much-worn-looking Bible. I was excited to meet another Christian in a place I was told held very few. Our conversation, however, changed my mind. While this man knew the letter of the Bible, having much of the Old Testament memorized, he was a long way from knowing the God who had written it. His words aimed at using verses out of context so that He could shut down our worship. His apparent anger aimed at our attempt to share the joy of the Lord did not come from a heart that understood the grace and truth of a loving Savior. I knew that until God broke through the hardness in his life, he would not be able to understand the mercy behind the words he quoted so well. I always say if what people are saying in the Bible say would not come out of the person of Jesus, they have misunderstood the Word of God.

    This experience and others helped me delay the reading of God's word until I become aware of His presence, for I need the fiery, passionate heart of God behind the words. His loving presence guides me to know the truth in a way that sets me free from using God's words to hurt myself and the people Jesus puts in my path each day. Remember when I wrote about the enemy getting in between intention and perception? He does this with scripture too. I have personally experienced the Bible used on me to do the opposite of God's intention, which is revealed in the context of a passage. My ex-husband used it to justify his affair and divorce, so I had a reason to divorce him; I used it to shame and dishonor him when I thought he wasn't spiritual enough. Both cases misused

Scripture. The practice of using God's words to justify hurtful behavior or to shame and wound others is one of the practices that must stop if our soul is to remain a home for Jesus.

What does this look like in my life? My bible remains closed on my lap until I have spent some time in worship of the God who wrote it. The best way to understand a book is to get to know the Author. Once I sense that connection, I open my Bible. As a rule, I have found it helpful to have a reading plan or book of the Bible as my go-to daily. Right now, I am reading First Peter as I study how Peter carried the presence of Jesus so well that people were healed as they came into his shadow. I want to live like that! I just finished a reading plan that took me through the gospels. However, either before or after I go there, I am learning to ask Jesus the question, "Where do you want me to read today"? I have had many days that I don't hear anything clearly, so I proceed to my normal daily reading. I am amazed at how God can have it be the perfect thing I need for that day, either for me or someone I run into. But on many occasions, I have had a specific scripture reference come into my mind. Usually, I have no idea what it is about. When I read it, I am always amazed at how it is the answer to some questions I am dealing with or the direction to a promise I desperately needed that day.

For example, not too long ago, I was spending a lot of my intercession time of prayer for my youngest son. He had some rough stuff in his life both because of both his choices and others. One specific night I felt the ache to see a turnaround in his life to bring the joy, hope, and success he needed. I sat down and grabbed my Bible, and asked the question, "Where should I read today?" Immediately I heard the thought, "Proverbs 13". Now, I wish I knew scripture enough to know what would be there, but I didn't. I must also say there was reluctance as I went to the book of Proverbs because, honestly, I didn't want another piece of the advice it often gives. But, in obedience to what I was sure was God's voice, I turned to that passage.

My jaw practically hit the page as I saw there, double-circled verse 12 with the name of my son written by it. I had circled it years earlier but had not remembered it was there, yet God did. The verse said, "Hope deferred makes the heart sick, but a dream fulfilled is a tree of life," each word flooded me with the hope I longed for. God had given me a promise I could both praise God for and declare towards that morning. In answer to the promise, by the end of that very day, my son had a new job, a new place to move to, and a new lease on life. This is one experience of many where God leads me when I go to His Word with the awareness of His presence.

Surrender, prayer, and reading God's word with awareness are the main areas I have seen God employ in my life as I seek to make my soul His home. My time spent in the living room of Jesus' presence being warmed by the fire of His word has led me into other practices as well. These include times of fasting and times of silence and solitude. I am often feeling the need to put on the armor of God written about in Ephesians 6: 10-18. These verses are filled with a powerful way God gave us to stand against our enemy, Satan, and the fallen angels sent to steal, kill, and destroy.[cxvi] I continue to use the Lord's Prayer Pattern, written by Armin Gesswein, to guide me on those days when I just can't find a place to begin.

Over the years that followed the move back to my hometown, that physical house slowly became a home. More importantly, Jesus has become at home in my soul more often than not. Once I surrendered to Him and gave Him an open door to my life, Jesus came in and went to work, making my soul a place full of His presence, full of His love, acceptance, protection, and hope. More and more, I am experiencing the truth expressed in Acts 17:28 confirms that as we make Jesus the home of our soul, "we live, and move, and have our being."

Chapter 8: A Soul Open to the Mess

"I always thought that the 'thriving' would come when everything was perfect, and what I learned is that it's actually down in the mess that things get good." - Joanna Gaines

"Without oxen a stable stays clean, but you need a strong ox for a large harvest." – Proverbs 14:4

The smell overwhelmed me. I knew there was mold there but could not figure out why. Even though recent heavy rain had seeped into our basement, leading to days of work and methods needed to dry it out, there must still be moisture somewhere. I had used the dry vacuum to get the water I could and had borrowed a heavy-duty fan to get rid of what I could not. The fan had been running 24/7 for over a week. The room appeared completely dry. So why was there not only the smell of mold but places I stepped in that were making my socks wet? As I examined the floor more carefully, I finally knew what I had to do, rip up these "waterproof" vinyl tiles one by one allowing air to access the cement below. As I pulled up the first tile, the problem became noticeably clear. Each tile was trapping water, water that had to be opened up to dry air. As each tile was removed, not only was the problem revealed, but a mess was made.

To Fix an Issue, It must be Revealed

It was clear that the only way to fix some issues is to open them up, to see what is lurking beneath or behind what you see. I couldn't just ignore the hidden water. I had to empty the room of its flooring so that the source of the problem could be dealt with. I have learned that this is also true when renovating the soul. God had started a great work of tearing down walls of self-protection and the door of fear I spoke about in previous chapters, but I soon discovered that there was clearly a stench of distrust in my life. It appears that no work of renovation is complete after the demo. Clean-up and putting new things back in place are necessary steps to complete restoration.

God had done considerable demos over the past years of my life, and now it was time for the clean-up process to begin. Just like the tile in my basement, each issue needed to be revealed and opened to see the source of my deepest problem of intimacy with God, fully trusting him enough to want to stay nearby. Rob Reimer explains it this way, "Many people come to me because they want to get closer to God, but they can't. What they fail to understand is that it is often soul issues that keep them from drawing near to God. Praying, fasting, and memorizing scripture cannot help us draw near unless we address the soul blocks. We have unconfessed, unprocessed, undealt with issues, and they hinder us from experiencing the fullness of God."[cxvii] You see, behind the walls of self-protection were issues that I had hidden there. Once concealed, now in plain sight. Thankfully, the atmosphere of openness is the only place soul issues can be dealt with.

Open space allows us to see clearly. To bring things into the light. When HGTV talks about an open concept, they are describing a floor plan that allows for clear sight lines and improved light. Dr. Reimer reminds us that "we cannot overcome that which we will not admit; light is a gift, it is not an intrusion."[cxviii] The pro about this is that with no walls to block your light, the beauty of your home is on full display. However, the con is that your whole mess is also on display. I believe that God wants to develop an "open concept" in our souls. This means I was and am going to learn to be authentic. You know, let people see the good, the bad, and the ugly. As my walls of self-protection came down, I found I could be open to a new way to react in this world. Open to ways I was never free to follow before when my walls were pulled down.

Opened up to critique

If I were superman, then criticism would have been my kryptonite. With little personal confidence and a whole lot of fear, fear of being exposed as the broken human being I was, I made defensiveness my weapon of choice. Defensiveness is a clear symptom of a lie believed. It was my default, my go-to way to make myself look okay, and it became as natural as coughing when you ingest smoke. As Gavin Ortlund puts it, "Nothing is more natural when we feel threatened by a criticism than to divert, distract, and downplay. It's as instinctive as flinching when a punch is coming".[cxix]

In response to the question, "what is the true meaning of defensiveness?" Columnist "Ask Ann" described it by saying, "People who are acting defensively are essentially trying to protect themselves from feeling a certain uncomfortable way, and from viewing themselves as a failure or otherwise in a negative light".[cxx] When criticism comes our way, it can quickly uphold our belief that we are not enough. A belief I certainly had until I fully let Jesus in, and he became my home. You see, Jesus showed me a whole different view of how to handle criticism. He showed me humility.

There are two passages of scripture that show us how to respond correctly to criticism. First, Matthew 26:62-63a, "Then the high priest stood up and said to Jesus, "Well, aren't you going to answer these charges? What do you have to say for yourself?" But Jesus remained silent". Yes, silent. Not a natural response but clearly the right one. So, I ask myself, what does silence accomplish? I find that as I learn to be silent when I am being criticized, it does two things. First, it helps me listen. If I jump to defend myself too quickly, I can miss the importance of what the person is saying. I can jump to conclusions that will end with never understanding what they are actually saying. Second, silence can let me separate out the truth of what is being said and the possible error in mine or their perception of the situation, giving way to a clear path to deal with the critique.

I remember one of the first times I decided to try this technique. I was visiting my adult daughter, and it soon became clear that she was working through some of the hurts she had as a result of the tumultuous marriage and divorce she witnessed as a teen. Her father was the first to get the brunt of her anger, and now it was my turn. As she began, my need to defend myself arose, but I invited Jesus into the situation and chose to just silently listen to the best of my ability. Though I could not stop the tears that the words caused to pour from my eyes, I wanted her to know that she was being heard. Both the truth of my mistakes and the power of the way she had perceived things brought me to the end of myself. I could not deny either. I could only apologize and hope for forgiveness, giving her the opportunity to vent any time she needed. We both found some healing that day, personally and in our relationship.

It is in the second passage of scripture that I found the strength to step back in those moments I want to defend myself. 1 Peter 2:23 talks about how Jesus handled the overwhelming condemnation he received on the way to the cross. It emphasizes, "He did not retaliate when he was insulted, nor threaten revenge when he suffered. *He left his case in the hands of God,* who always judges fairly" [Emphasis mine]. When I leave my case in God's hands, all I am left to do is repent. For both the truth of what I did and the way my actions hurt the other person. Because I have the indwelling Holy Spirit and have found my identity in Christ, I can be open to hearing the hard stuff. Open to honestly confronting my own sinful behavior and confronting the hurt it causes. Gavin Ortlund, in his article, *Repentance vs. Defensiveness,* goes on to say, "The gospel alone can free us for honesty, ownership, and admission because the gospel alone destroys the sting and judgment associated with criticism. The gospel takes away the fear that drives defensiveness and frees us to openly admit our shortcomings".[cxxi]

As I now work with people in my *Finding Home Soul Care* ministry, I help them find Jesus as the home for their souls. I may be confronted by those who get hurt by my actions or lack of action. But Jesus' example and influence in my life make being open to criticism possible. Not only possible but a necessary part of a healthy environment. Openness to criticism leads to another necessary openness. With every confrontation, we must remain open to experiencing conflict.

Opened up to Conflict

My father's name was Fred which literally means "peaceful ruler". That is a perfect description of who he was. Peace was a particularly important environment in my home growing up. His quiet and gentle heart struggled with conflict of any kind, and it became his mission to keep the peace. A mission I saw him live out all his days. I learned the importance of peace from him, but I did not learn how to handle conflict in a healthy way. I learned how to push back my feelings behind a wall in order to keep the peace. Behind that wall was a dam ready to burst. And a burst of emotions always hurts everyone around. Even though I thought I was keeping the peace, I was really just experiencing the façade of peace, and eventually, it caused pain instead of peace.

Keeping the peace is a wonderful goal when we go about it correctly. I mean, we are called to be peacemakers (Matthew 5:9), but I tried to avoid conflict by stuffing my feeling and attitudes deep within. Though outer conflict seems to be circumvented, I was left with a stress-filled inner conflict instead. Keeping the peace at any cost meant giving up more and more of myself. My life was spent with a "walking on eggshell" kind of existence that led to the continued destruction of my soul. This false peace will not do what peace is supposed to do; make us more like Christ and more of who He made us to be. Matthew 5:9 clarifies that the way to show we are children of God is down the path of peacemaking.

Our English word "peace" is a passive picture, showing the absence of hostility and strife. However, the biblical concept of peace is bigger than that. The Bible Dictionary state that "[peace] rests heavily on the Hebrew root *slm*, which means "to be complete" or "to be sound." The verb conveys both a dynamic and a static meaning" to be complete or whole" or "to live well."[cxxii] That is the kind of peace worth pursuing, a peace worth fighting for.

    I recently talked to my friend, who is a middle school boys' basketball coach. He, like my dad, strives to develop a peace-filled environment for his team. At his last practice, one of the boys came in with an attitude that could only be described as disruptive. My friend wrestled with how to maintain peace. Should he avoid conflict by just letting the boy be a part of the activities that day, knowing that it would affect the attitudes and performance of the others? Or should he confront the boy and give him a choice to change his attitude or leave? Both choices seemed to go against his desire to keep the peace. But the latter would assure that peace would rule during that practice. It would take confrontation to achieve peace which can seem like an oxymoron.

    As we long to have peace in our souls, we must, at times, confront the issues getting in the way of that peace. Keeping a peaceful space in our souls means practicing the presence of the Prince of Peace within me. We must look into the Gospels to learn how Jesus handled conflict. The gospel of Matthew gives us some clear indications of how Jesus showed us how to handle conflict to maintain and create peace. I saw four ways Jesus shows us how to handle conflict.

    First, Jesus tells us to confront the problem quickly. He clarifies that in the case of having a problem with a friend, "abandon your offering, leave immediately, go to this friend and make things right. Then and only then, come back and work things out with God". The fact is that peace does not come because of just waiting long enough to let things settle. Though spending time in God's presence first is important to get his view on the issue, when there is a clear indication, you need to go and confront the issue head-on with love, grace, and humility.

My track record on this one is not so good. I can try to confuse it with my issues of fear and anxiety, but in truth, I just didn't want others to know I was wrong. That sounds a lot like pride, a most deadly sin. For a long time, I just thought that not talking about issues or just letting the other person win was the best way to keep the peace. This cost me dearly in my first marriage and with my kids. Unresolved or ignored conflict both beat my soul up and let my kids down. I have learned that we must develop healthy boundaries in our souls to deal with conflicts. The book *Boundaries for Your Soul*[cxxiii] gives three great suggestions about what to do when confronting conflict.

1. Invite Jesus to come near and hand over your fear and receive peace in exchange

2. Recruit this peaceful part to advise you about how to speak to the person intentionally instead of reactively.

3. Communicate your feelings and requests lovingly to the other.

The second way Jesus tells us to handle conflict is to do it face to face. In Matthew 18:15, he says, "If a fellow believer hurts you, go and tell him—work it out between the two of you". It is amazing how looking into someone's eyes will affect how you achieve peace. I do believe that a person's eyes will tell you a lot about how they hear you and how their soul is responding to your words. As mirrors to the soul, you will soon see if peace is developing or not. In this age of text and Facebook messaging, we often miss the power of the story that can be seen in a face.

      I know for a fact that face-to-face matters, but it is hard. That is why so much of the tension between people is often done through text, email, and, sadly, for the world to see on Facebook. Even emojis can lead us to misunderstanding. Truthfully, I find anything other than face-to-face confrontation cowardly. My past defensiveness probably made it even harder to confront me face to face. Maybe that is why my ex-husband chose to tell me all of the reasons he was leaving via email. I think he found it much easier to say cruel words when he didn't have to look at me. When you don't have to see the reaction, you can let your venting have full use of the language that a reacting face would have steered down a gentler path. My defensiveness may be why my adult children use email and text to let me know they are angry at my views. Now, with my defensiveness gone, I have sought to let them know that I am a safe place to vent their frustrations. My love will withstand any of their strong opinions thrown my way. My hope is that by communicating face-to-face, we will learn to hear each other's hearts and protect each other's souls.

      The third way Jesus shows us how to create peace out of conflict is in the second part of Matthew 18:15. This resolving of conflict must be done "between the two of you". I have found that embarrassment will never get you on the road to peace. When you are out of the earshot of those who can influence the conversation, you are more likely to hear the soul of the person you are against. The important thing to remember is that before you go to that person, you must have a one-on-one conversation with Jesus. Ask to see his perspective of the situation. Ask him to reveal where you are wrong and need to come clean about and apologize. Get wisdom on how to accomplish the peace God desires. Then no matter the outcome of the encounter with that person, you will know you did all that God has required of you and can leave the rest to him.

My experience with the importance of the privacy of conflict came in experiencing the consequences of the opposite approach. I was completely devastated when my ex-husband decided to email my entire family his list of grievances with me. Not only was most of it only his side of the story, but the picture it painted left me full of shame. I believe that we have lost the art of private confrontation. Social media makes it so much easier to air your dirty laundry for all to see. We can enjoy getting others on our side because we can feel vindicated that we were right. Yet, truth is lost in the darkness of "likes". Real peace comes when two people can sit down, and both speak and listen to each other's hearts, confess, forgive and move into deeper respect and relationship together or with a trusted Counselor/Pastor.

Last, Jesus wants us to get help. Verses 16 and 17 of Matthew 18 let us know that we may not be able to achieve peace on our own. He shows us the progress by starting one on one, then, if not resolved, going to two or three otherwise people and eventually a larger group of people who are helpers. I have found that coming together with mutual friends or even wise leadership can direct me to find ways to approach conflict in the best way possible. Yet, this passage shows that sometimes peace cannot be achieved. However, it never says to avoid it. The key to finding peace in the home of your soul is to make every effort to show love, humility, and mercy in order to bring peace into the situation. If that does not work, we can simply pray for them as the Prince of Peace follows them out the door of your life.

I remember a group of friends who did this for me. It was back when my children were in preschool, kindergarten, and second grade. I was homeschooling and working evenings. Life was overwhelming, and I was making some unhealthy choices. Basically, I was letting my depression guide my eating habits, and the consequences were obvious. One of my friends decided to point it out. My pride hurt; I stopped all communication with her. Thankfully, she had learned how to follow the Matthew 18 principles. Soon a few of my friends invited me to join them for lunch. When I showed up, she was there too. Yet somehow, they were able to both listen to my heart and speak the healing truth. That wonderful friend, who cared enough to intervene, is one of my favorite people to this day.

I have learned the truth that conflict is inevitable. Gary Smalley wrote that "Any person involved in a sustained relationship is bound to experience conflict with that other person eventually. It's a part of getting to know and adjusting to a person, his or her habits, values, and ways of functioning. Two people will never have the same expectations, thoughts, opinions or needs".[cxxiv] But that does not mean that peace is not worth seeking. Since Jesus is the embodiment of peace, when he lives in the home of our soul, we can live in peace and bring peace into every situation, even if that means dealing with conflict. Living with a peaceful open soul will allow you to be you instead of hiding behind the conflict.

Opened up to Real Emotions

The problem with the open door policy in the home of your soul is that it is hard to hide stuff. Right now, as I type, I can see into our living room where all the dog toys are lying on the floor and a ripped-up sock I didn't know he took. With no door to shut off that room, the chaos of dog ownership is clearly visible. Yet the reality of them being there means that I have a loving pup that I adore. I understand that the chaos he creates is just part of being a dog, and that helps me handle it. Sometimes, to have an open soul is to be open to the chaos of being human.

As I study the life of Jesus, I see Him repeatedly showing us his humanness. Jesus never hid the fact that he was not just fully God, but He was fully man. He felt his emotions strongly, solidly, and authentically. Jesus let us know that he got tired. In John chapter 4, we find that the reason Jesus stopped at the well where he met the Samaritan woman was that he was weary. Jesus didn't hide his anger when he turned the tables as he entered the temple in Matthew 21. He didn't hide his frustration at his disciples' lack of faith when he said, "O unbelieving and perverse generation," Jesus replied, "how long shall I stay with you and put up with you?"[cxxv] There was no hiding the tears he shed at Lazarus' tomb[cxxvi] or the loss he felt as he heard of the death of his cousin John.[cxxvii] I can only deduce that hiding our true emotions is not living like Jesus.

His example shows that showing real emotions are okay and, at the same time, makes sure not to be led by those emotions. Emotions are part of the way we were created. It is part of being in the image of God. Emotions, when well processed, can be an environment for a healthy soul. Here is what I discovered in my counseling training, what you feel comes directly from what you think and what you feel will determine your behavior. In technical terms, this is called cognitive-behavioral therapy. The key to changing behavior is to change your feeling, which can only be changed by what you think. This is why processing your emotions is key to a healthy soul.

The best way I have found to do this is to get the emotion outside yourself and look at it from a different perspective. I often use an object that I name the emotion I am processing. For instance, I will grab a doll from my kid's collections still in my basement. I would name it, for instance, Anxiety. Then I would look at it and ask the following questions as if talking to the doll. Are you helping or hurting? If helping, then why? If hurting, then why? What thought is causing you to be here? Maybe I am thinking I am not worthy or good enough. Then I ask, is that thought true? If true, what should I do about it? If not true, what do I know about who I am in Christ that counters that lie? When I discover the truth and choose to hold on to the truth, I have more control of my feeling and, therefore, my behavior. Ignoring the feeling will never help you change the thinking that is leaving a mess in your soul. I try to take time every morning or evening and process my emotions in the presence of Jesus because I discovered that even my mess of my emotions couldn't stop his love and his willingness to help us find the truth. In fact, we can start to feel His love more and more as we see Him actively helping us clean up our souls.

Yes, having an open, authentic soul will be messy, but in the mess of clean-up, we will get to the real issues stinking up our souls. Opening up your soul to critique can reveal the truth that will set you free. Opening up yourself to a healthy conflict will bring the aroma of peace. Plus, opening up yourself to your real emotions can transform the way your soul feels. It will start to feel more like home.

Chapter 9: A Soul at Home is Always Alert

"Life has its woes so learn to be on your toes, be alert." — Bernard Kelvin Clive

"It is like a man away on a journey… assigning to each one his task, also commanded the doorkeeper to stay on the alert." – Mark 13:34

The house was quiet and cool on a hot summer day. My sweet pup was sound asleep next to me. As revealed in the calmness around me and sat petting his brown and white fur. Dinner was finished, and all cleaned up. With my new favorite Netflix series playing in the background, I allowed the tensions of the day to melt away. All was well in my world at that moment. Until… Crowder, my sweet Springer Spaniel, jumped up with a bark and a growl. I had not heard anything, but he did. Off to the window, he ran loudly, barking along the way. With curiosity, I got up and followed him to see what had interrupted our cuddle time. Out on the street, two of his favorite humans and their two dogs, his best friends, were passing quite close to the house. He had reacted to a potential threat, and now he wanted to go out and play because there were friends outside to interact with. Due to the alertness of my four-legged companion, we both found something better to do, be with those we could care for.

I can get very self-involved. The world outside my window does not enter my thoughts much. I have slept through storms and missed incredible rainbows. This self-focus keeps me from seeing beyond my four walls to the wonder outside my front door. This can be true personally, too. I can be so inside my own head I can miss countless important moments.

The more I let Jesus influence my soul, the more I have learned that it is far more important to pay attention to what is going on outside of myself. I need to give the inner workings of my soul to Him and trust Him. When I do, I can, with those dog-like senses, be alert to the tasks I have been assigned to carry out each day.

Jesus was a great example of what living alert looks like. The Gospels are full of examples of Jesus being alert to the heart of those around him. In Luke 19:5, Jesus saw more than just a man in a tree and knew what Zacchaeus' heart needed most of all. Zacchaeus needed Jesus to be in his home, and so I am sure his heart did a leap when Jesus said, "Quick, come down! I must be a guest in your home today." Back in Mark 6, it records the feeding of the 5000 where the disciples only saw the problem of a mass of hungry people, but Jesus "saw the huge crowd as he stepped from the boat, and he had compassion on them because they were like sheep without a shepherd". [cxxviii] And in Mark 10, Jesus sees beyond the outward façade of the young rich man to the heart of his issue, and so "Jesus looked at him and loved him." Love that wanted to be with this desperate man when He told him, "Come, follow me."[cxxix]

In the stories above, we glean how Jesus teaches us not to just be stuck fixing our own souls but relying on the Holy Spirit living there to notice more, to hear other's souls. In the book *Listen, Love, Repeat,* Karen Ehman says, "We need to live alert, listening for heart drops, those "read between the lines" gut-level feelings we have about someone's needs based on really trying to listen to their heart".[cxxx] We can't do that stuck in our own heads or focused just on our own souls. I spent too many years doing just that, and all my soul revealed was hurt and pain. Once I started living with Jesus as my soul's home and let Him focus on my heart, the less I was buried under the weight of my own pain, and the more I could feel compassion for the pain in the souls of others. There are three ways that the practice of living alert will make a difference. It helps you see, listen and help others more intentionally.

Living Alert Helps You See Others

Karen Ehman put it best when she wrote, "We need to learn to see beyond ourselves and our lives and into the pain of others. We must make this a matter of prayer, asking God to increase our sensitivity to what others are thinking and feeling.[cxxxi] I have seen God do this for me on numerous occasions. I remember going with a friend to help a woman named Terri clean out her apartment. As we opened the door, our eyes understood the reason she was struggling with this move. Piles and piles of clothes, dishes, magazines, and more were everywhere. My natural mind started to go critical, but the Holy Spirit directed soul sensed something else as I prayed for strength. The compassion of God flooded my soul, and it made all the difference that day. Not only did I have the energy needed to complete the task, but Jesus also helped me see a woman with a wounded soul trying to fill that hole with things. Things that were doing the opposite of what she needed. My renewed attitude to her opened that door to a relationship that is leading her closer to Jesus, the soul filler. I am helping her find Jesus as her soul's home.

There have been so many times in my battle with the chronic pain of fibromyalgia, an invisible illness, that I wanted someone to see that I was hurting. I longed for them to notice the ache of my soul instead of the normalness of my outward appearance. The ones that did were the ones who suffered too. They had learned from the constant presence of Jesus in their souls to notice more. The more I make it a practice to practice His presence, the more I am aware of those who need more of Him. I am so encouraged by the story in the Bible of the woman with the bleeding issue that sought to touch the hem of Jesus' garment to find healing. The disciples were blinded by the crowd, but Jesus turned to see her. To look in her eyes and make her feel seen.[cxxxii]

We must do the same for others. We must stop and turn from the crowds. Those crowded thoughts, crowded worries, and crowded schedules to see the hurting souls besides us. Turn to them and let them know we see them. See the hurt, see the sadness, see the broken places and encourage them with the love of the Jesus we serve. We must create the same atmosphere of home we have found in our souls so those we encounter feel seen and therefore accepted, significant and safe. For me, it means putting down my phone and deleting the apps that take my focus away. It means being in that persistent prayer[cxxxiii] the Bible refers to, so I am ready to respond to the prompts of the Holy Spirit, showing me who He sees at that moment. Then I must turn and see them with eyes that notice those "heart drops" to clue us on how we can love and nourish their soul. Yet, seeing is just the beginning and must move us to listen to their souls too.

Living Alert Helps You Listen.

One of the most convicting quotes I have heard is by Stephen R. Covey, who said, "Most people do not listen with the intent to understand; they listen with the intent to reply." Yep, that second part was always me. I was the classic interrupter. I have a reply way before someone is finished talking, and my impatience usually doesn't let them finish. That conviction started me thinking about my need to change that behavior. Yet, it was the realization of how much I longed to be heard that told me that others must feel like that too.

The turnaround came when I was kindly told that I said, "Do you know what I mean?" over and over in my conversations with people. At first, I didn't believe it; I mean, I had never heard myself say it. I was determined to listen for it and prayed that God would let me hear myself talk. Wow, I did say it all the time without realizing it. Habit, I guess, but why? The answer was right there in the statement. I wanted to be heard and understood. My lack of confidence in what I was saying came out every time I had to ask a question. Once I heard it, I found myself making myself stop, but I also realized I was so busy trying to be heard I had lost the art of listening to understand others.

During that season of readjusting my listening abilities, I also started reading the New Testament, and I noticed that Jesus repeatedly asked those he was speaking to if they heard Him and if they were listening. Even God the Father told the disciples at the transfiguration to listen to his son. [cxxxiv] The most repeated phrase in the book of Revelation is "anyone who has ears to hear, must listen to what the Spirit is saying…" [cxxxv] Clearly, hearing and listening are two different levels, and listening is a must.

The difference is that hearing is one of our five senses. It "is the act of perceiving sound and receiving sound waves or vibrations through your ear" [cxxxvi]. On the other hand, listening takes a concentrated effort with the goal of understanding what you hear. You don't have to be quiet for the former, but you should be for the latter. If you choose, like I have, to live alert, it is imperative to learn the art of "listening to understand." Groups like AA and Celebrate Recovery always have their group sharing times as a listen, do not respond rule. Not only does this help those working towards the recovery process, but it also helps them gain active listening skills. In my women's soul care groups, I ask those who attend to pay attention to who is speaking with eye contact, leaning into what they are saying. I ask them to put aside distractions like texting (basically putting away their cell phones) and keep from thinking up their next response. It is the way to make sure these hurting women are feeling valued. As I counsel, I always have a paper and pencil to mark down thoughts so I can continue to listen with intent and care. Being distracted can be one of the most disrespectful and hurtful ways to cause others soul pain.

Living alert in your soul is about being present and listening to the heart of the person you are with. Krista Tippett is a Peabody Award-winning broadcaster and a New York Times bestselling author who has an excellent talk on The Art of Generous Listening.[cxxxvii] In it, she said, "Listening is about being present, not just about being quiet." I know that I can be quiet yet far away in my thoughts, daydreaming of something quite removed from my current setting. Active listening is being quiet so you can pay attention to what is going on right now, at that moment. This kind of living makes the home environment we are creating feel safe and will nourish the soul of the one speaking.

When we listen with an ear to the Holy Spirit, we don't just hear the spoken words. We will often hear the unspoken ones. As Karen Ehman shares, "My desire is not just to hear the words spoken but to hear the unspoken heart words as well.[cxxxviii] Once you have learned to hear the heart's words, souls are brought closer to Jesus, who lives in your soul. It helps them find a home for their soul to feel accepted, significant and safe. When your soul is home with Jesus, there soon, the souls of those around you can be transformed to have that too. Jesus in your soul will transform the world around you.

Chapter 10: Where Jesus Dwells, Love Dwells

"What does love look like? It has the hands to help others. It has the feet to hasten to the poor and needy. It has eyes to see misery and want. It has ears to hear the sighs and sorrows of men. That is what love looks like." -St Augustine

"And walk in love, as Christ loved us and gave himself up for us, a fragrant offering and sacrifice to God." – Ephesians 5:2

As I walked up to the house, my mind was spinning. Would they look at me differently? Was I an embarrassment now? Shame on the family name. Should I hide my wounded soul or let the ugliness of it all pour out? Would they look away or possibly look right at me in judgment? This would be the first time I would be visiting my brother's family since the divorce. There was no good reason to think those thoughts, yet the loudness of them was hard for me to ignore. That is until the first person I connected with on the other side of that door created an environment of the one thing I desperately needed, love. The look in my nephew Nathan's eyes reflected the deep sadness of compassion for what I had been going through. His hug reassured me that rejection was not even a possibility. I knew that I remained, despite my circumstances, a beloved member of his family. The loving atmosphere that Nathan carried led me to find the love of Jesus in my soul.

When Jesus is Your Home, You Will Love Like Him

I believe the reason Nathan could love so well is that since childhood, he was passionate about living like Jesus. He had truly grasped the truth that Jesus loved him so he could love others well. He chose to make Jesus his soul's home and spent time dwelling in the Gospel accounts of the life of Jesus. There he saw that Jesus' life and death demonstrated the kind of love God had created; love that is unconditional, sacrificial, and forgiving. As he let that kind of love dwell in his heart through his relationship with Jesus, he was able to love others in the same way leading many to find Jesus as their soul's home. Nathan, at the age of 30, gave his life while saving the life of a young teen he pastored. Though we all miss him terribly, we are inspired to pursue a life of letting our souls be immersed in the love of Jesus and living in such a way that loving others are a natural flow.

As I have spent time immersing myself in the Gospels, I see that Jesus so clearly demonstrated how to create a loving home-like atmosphere wherever he walked. In story after story, I perceived how Jesus reestablished what love was meant to be, not how humanity had tainted it, and gave us a clear example of how it should look every day. I am not necessarily talking about John 3:16 love, a love only the supernatural God can exhibit. Though it is absolutely true that "God demonstrates his own love for us in this: While we were still sinners, Christ died for us," I am always looking for the ways that God calls us to love like the Jesus who dwells in our souls. Living like Jesus in the everyday encounters that come on our journey of life.

To figure out what living like Jesus looks I made Him the supreme focus of my life. I dove into scripture to see what He did day to day and how it could look to live it personally and express the kind of love Jesus has for His world. I started in Matthew 1:1 and read all the way to John 21:25 repeatedly.

I was so amazed at the clarity it gave me to see some very practical ways Jesus walked out His love and, in that, made people feel at home in their souls. Revealed in every story, we see who Jesus is and how He was the home we all can live in and emulate. His attitudes and choices are the building materials as our soul cares for the souls of others.

For my purposes in this book, I have pulled out three specific traits about Jesus revealed in scripture that showed that He carried the answers to people's biggest needs for home and then a few specific choices He made that demonstrated them. I believe that because Jesus both dwelt in the love of His Father and relied on the Holy Spirit, he could be accepting, show people they are significant, and make them feel safe. Jesus was always listening to people's cries for help and encouraging them in the way that they could live with Him forever. Those people learned how to make Jesus their soul's home and then lead others to Him for an opportunity to have all Christ offers. If we learn to dwell deeply in the love of our God the Father and rely on the Holy Spirit, we can do the works that Jesus did and make the atmosphere of home a common experience in this world.

Jesus Is: A Home Filled with Acceptance

Every human being has a longing to be accepted, to not be rejected for who we are. Neil Anderson puts it this way "Our need for acceptance and belonging are legitimate needs. They are God-given. But if we attempt to meet them independent of God, we are doomed to reap the dissatisfaction the self-life brings"[cxxxix] We were created to be just who God made us to be and loved because of it. Yet, over and over in life, people reject and ostracize us instead of treating us with the respect God desires for us. When this rejection happens over and over, we start believing that we do not deserve respect and acceptance. Our souls will either reject everyone as a form of protection or do everything, no matter how bad, to try to gain acceptance. Both of which will leave our souls homeless and overwhelmed.

The good news is that Jesus accepts us where we are, no matter what. We never have to change for Jesus to love us. Then as we make Him our soul's home, he works in us to do all we need to truly be who He made us to be. There are quite a few stories in the Bible that show that Jesus accepts those He is with. Let's look at one of my favorites. It takes place at a well outside Samaria.

Jesus is tired, and he sends the disciples to get some supplies. Jacob's well is right there, and it was a good place to rest. A Samaritan woman came to get water and was surprised when a Jewish man talked to her. The Bible records her response. "The Samaritan woman said to him, "You are a Jew, and I am a Samaritan woman. How can you ask me for a drink? (For Jews do not associate with Samaritans)."[cxl] If anyone were unacceptable, it would be a woman who is Samaritan. On top of that, she was a woman with multiple marriages and was not married to who she was with now. This had left her rejected and ostracized. Yet, Jesus sees her value as one who is worthy of His time. Through His acceptance of her on that hot day, it changed her and the world around her forever. This shows me no matter how rejected we have been, Jesus will accept you and then, through you change the world. Remember, "when you know who you are in Christ, you no longer need to be threatened by people or compete with them because you are already secure and loved."[cxli] You are already accepted by the only One who truly matters. Jesus is your home of acceptance.

Jesus Is: A Home Full of Significance

Significance is another one of our six core needs. Why? Because we were created by God to do significant things and be unique and needed, mainly because He says we are. So significant, in fact, that Jesus died a sinner's death to make sure you can live forever with Him. You can't get more significant than that. Yet, we try to find out significance in two ways that never work. We try to feel significant by who we know, what we do, and how we do it. But none of these will lead to true significance.

First of all, we will try to find significance in the leader we follow. How many times did I find my significance in letting people know that I was my brother Randy's sister because people highly respected him? It seemed to work when I followed him to college initially until it didn't, and I had to, and, to me, I wasn't enough. Paul in 1 Corinthians 3:1 rebuked those who were trying to get their significance by who they followed. He said, "When one of you says, 'I follow Paul,' and another says, 'I follow Apollos,' aren't you acting just like people of the world?" (vs. 4). Paul goes on to let them know that "we are both God's workers" (vs.9). They were holding on to a lie and Paul needed them to understand the truth. Our significance comes from being in Christ and part of His family. We are all God's workmanship, no one more significant than another.

Second, we try to find our significance in our own self-effort. Being God's workers means He has a plan to accomplish much through us. The problem becomes when we believe the lie that it is in what we do that makes us significant. This leads us to try to do everything with our own strength. Many, like me, were actually taught growing up in the church that it is what we do that makes us Christian. A dangerous lie that has poisoned many to walk away from the church and Jesus. We must turn and understand that it is Christ in us that accomplishes anything. His work makes us significant. How much can we achieve without Him? Nothing. Remember what John 15:5 says? "Apart from [Jesus Christ], you can do nothing." Our significance lies in Christ's work, not ours. It is not what we do but what Christ did that makes us significant.

      The Bible tells of someone who was trying to find significance in themselves, and yes, it is the same Paul that wrote the verses I mentioned. As Saul, a leader in the church, he was proud of who he knew and what he did. When Jesus entered his life, all that changed. In Acts 22, Paul tells his story of finding significance. "I am a Jew, born in Tarsus in Cilicia, but brought up in this city, educated at the feet of Gamaliel according to the strict manner of the law of our fathers, being zealous for God as all of you are this day. I persecuted this Way to the death, binding and delivering to prison both men and women" (vs. 3,4). Yet, an encounter with Jesus showed Paul where his significance came from. "'The God of our fathers has appointed you to know His will, and to see the Righteous One, and to hear His voice. You will be His witness to everyone of what you have seen and heard" (vs. 14,15). Paul realized that it is his relationship with Jesus that makes him significant, and you should too. Jesus is your home of significance.

Jesus Is: A Home that is Secure

The home I just moved into came with a security doorbell system. Both the insurance company and my husband and I were thankful for it. Why? Because it makes us feel safe. We can see who comes to the door, whether we are there or not. It gives us notifications if there is movement at the door, and we can check to see what it is. I could even talk to someone who came to our door when I was away. I love this because I want to be and feel secure. According to Maslow's Hierarchy of Needs, we have to feel safe before we can feel loved and respected.[cxlii] Thankfully, God has declared that as His child, we are secure. Proverbs 3:23 tells us that "you will go your way in safety, and your foot will not stumble" because you are God's son or daughter.

Enter Satan, your enemy. Safe is the last thing he wants you to feel. Fear is his goal for you. So afraid, we feel as if we believe his lies instead of the truth of our security in Christ. Fear leads us to try to find our security in false places. We say, "maybe if we have enough money, we will be safe" or "being married will give me safety" However, we will never find security that lasts in finances or in temporal relationships.

If you depend on your money to keep you safe, I wonder if you have actually watched the news lately. Neil Anderson wrote that "I believe that the financial structures of this world are being shaken to their very core. Who can predict with confidence where the money markets of this world will be in the next few years"[cxliii] If you are reading this book after 2022, you may already know. The real question is, "what are you content with?"

1 Timothy 6 talks about this when Paul mentions "godliness with contentment" being of "great gain." Paul says

what should we should be content with. "But if we have food and clothing, we will be content with that." (vs. 8). Yet, Jesus says in Matthew 6, "Therefore I tell you, do not worry about your life, what you will eat or drink; or about your body, what you will wear. Is not life more than food, and the body more than clothes?" (v. 25). He can say this because as you seek Him and His kingdom "all these things will be added to you" (v. 33).

When my first husband had an affair and divorced me, I learned that security is never in a temporal relationship. Insecurity and loss are the results of depending on relationships in this life to give you your security. Every relationship on this side of eternity is temporary. They can end in death, rejection, or simply a move. It is always dangerous to let an earthly relationship replace God as our source of security. It is also dangerous to let depending on yourself for security be your answer to fear.

The Bible reveals how people can rely on something other than Jesus to find safety. Matthew 8:23-27 tells the story of the disciples of Jesus in a boat during an intense story. As the storm broke out, the disciples quickly realized that the boat was not going to keep them safe, nor was their skill as a fisherman. Fear led them to forget who was in the boat with them. We know this because Jesus rebuked them, saying, "You of little faith, why are you so afraid?" (v. 26). I would have said, "um, the storm, the waves, everyone that is not helping in the boat." But Jesus did not need an excuse. He needed simple trust in who was with them. Jesus is the only source of true safety even in the middle of the storms of life. If He is in your soul, you will get to the other side of every storm, whether he calms it or not. Jesus is your home of security.

Therefore, Jesus, as the center of your soul, is the answer to your acceptance, significance, and security. Choosing to make Him your home base will affect every situation you have faced and will face. This book has shown you ways to make Jesus your home. As you look to Jesus, He will help fix your foundation of identity and forgiveness. Jesus will remove the obstacles of self-protection, believed lies, and fear. Jesus will be with you in the mess and help you live alert to those around you that need Him. He wants to be your home forever and ever. Let Jesus be your soul's home. Move in with Him today. There is only one more step in that process. Let Jesus maintain the home every day for the rest of your life.

Chapter 11: Conclusion – Maintenance Required

"When the smoke detector goes off, you fix it. You don't buy a new home" - Anonymous

"But as for you, continue in the things you have learned and firmly believed..." – 2 Timothy 3:14

As you walk up to my house, you will see a front porch with chairs for sharing. Through the front door is vaulted ceilings, wood beams, a stone fireplace, and two sliding glass doors looking onto a yard with room to have some fun. Corn fields and mature trees are in your view as you sit in the living room. The master bedroom is quite roomy and is attached to a bathroom, complete with a large jetted tub and walk-in shower with body jets that soothe the stiffness of aging body parts. There is no clear way to tell you how this house became mine except as a gift from my good God. It took what I consider miracles to be writing at the island counter today.

I see redemption in every corner of this home. You see, when my first marriage ended after 16 years, I lost the dream house I described in chapter one. Now, after 16 amazing years with the love of my life, God gave me a dream home back. However, it is my dream home mainly because of who lives here. My Doug, who loves me well, and Jesus, who gives me identity, acceptance, significance, and security, live here. All these earthly things around me could be gone tomorrow, but not my Jesus. He is my everlasting dream home. Jesus is the only forever home.

Yet, I have learned that even the greatest homes need maintenance. We have only lived here a few months and have already had to fix some issues that are causing problems. Every earthly thing will be in need of repair or replacement. As long as we live on this side of eternity, our home with Jesus will need maintenance too. In both homes, there are leaks, breakdowns, and normal wear and tear. If I don't keep on top of these issues, eventually, the home becomes unlivable. Our home has had three main problems so far, and they have all involved leaking water. Leaking is also an issue in the home of my soul.

Water Leaks, Even Living Water

Wherever there is water, there will eventually be leaks. Water is really good at making its way through every crack and crevice provided. One of the first places I found a leak in our new home was as I was cleaning up the basement where my friends' kids had been playing during their visit. A toy had landed on my treadmill in the corner of the room, and as I picked it up, I noticed that it was wet. After a debate in my head about which of those children could have done this, I was hit by a drop of water on my head. Looking up, I saw the culprit. The wood was wet in streaks, and all this was pooling into a slow drip that landed on anything below it.

The wood above my head was beneath that incredible shower I had just enjoyed that morning. How could something recently remodeled leak already? Well, because that is what happens to all earthly things. Again, I say, where there is water, there will be leaks. Water is a powerful force in this world. It wears away rocks, one of the hardest substances there are. It turns out it had worn through the grout used to seal the shower pan. Now the water had made its way out and onto the beams and floor below it.

Jesus lives in us through the Holy Spirit, whom he poured out in power on the day of Pentecost (Acts 2). The Bible says He was "poured out" because Jesus refers to the Holy Spirit as living water. "If anyone thirsts, let him come to Me and drink. He who believes in Me, as the Scripture has said, out of his heart will flow rivers of living water" (John 7:37–38). It is the water of the Holy Spirit that makes us feel the closeness to Jesus that we long for. The Holy Spirit is our source of the abundant life Jesus promised in John 10:10. Abundant life is only available as we access the fruit of the Holy Spirit; love, joy, peace, patience, kindness, goodness, faithfulness, gentleness, and self-control (Galatians 5:22-23). Yet, because we live in a sin-filled world, that living water will leak. David Jerimiah writes, "I think it is safe to say that a Christian can experience the power of the Spirit draining out of his life. And like the vast majority of leaks in literal water systems, leaks in our spiritual reservoirs happen beneath the surface, out of sight, one drip–drip–drip at a time—until we realize we have lost all power or spiritual health."[cxliv]

Just as the leak in my shower is causing the wood in our floor's support system to become rotted, the leaking of the Holy Spirit can cause the rotting of your soul's support system. A rotted soul soon becomes a homeless soul. It is imperative to find the why of the leak, so we know how to repair it. The leak in my shower came from poor drainage and a crack in its protective covering. The leaks in our soul come from similar sources, and knowing the tools that will repair them keeps your soul's home maintained.

The Leakage Issue of Expectations

I expected my new home to be perfect. I mean, it looked just like I wanted it to. However, I soon discovered that even a dream home has issues. The shower leak brought me back to reality. Lysa Terkeurst, in her book *Its Not Supposed to Be This Way,* wrote, "The human heart was created in the context of the perfection of the garden of Eden. But we don't live there now... And we are epically disappointed." [cxlv] Expectations are dangerous things. I can expect my home with Jesus to look a certain way, too; you know, perfect. Yet, we must remember that Jesus is in control, not us. Our key to a home with Jesus is surrender. We also must remember that Jesus' will and ways are way above ours and come from a completely perspective; eternal.

Each time we put expectations on how our life with Jesus should look, we will be, as Lysa said, "epically disappointed." Disappointment causes leaks in our souls, and we can start to lose the power of the Holy Spirit in us. I suffered from constant grief because my expectations of Jesus did not line up with His plans, and therefore, I felt I was always losing my dreams. In fact, I thought God was a God who dangled good things in front of me only to pull them away when I was counting on them. This view of God created a large crack in my soul, and I could not hold on to the abundant life that His living water gives. This crack in my soul is an issue that needs an immediate fix.

I found the tool I needed to fix the leak of expectations. Purposely learning who God is through a study of His names will fix my view of God so I can have more realistic expectations. Our *Father of Mercies and the God is the God of all Comfort* (2 Corinthians 1:3) because Jesus tells us that "in this world you will have trouble" (John 16:33). God is *Jehovah Jireh* (Genesis 22:14), our provider because we sin and free will leaves us in a needy environment. God is *The God Ready to Forgive* (Nehemiah 9:17) because we are sinners who desperately need forgiveness. He is on the edge of His seat, ready to provide. Plus, *God is Love* (1 John 4:8); that is literally His name which is how He can send Jesus to die for us "while we were still sinners" (Romans 5:8).

As I know God by His names, I understand that He cannot purposely disappoint us. It is Satan that plants the lie so we can lose our only source of joy and contentment and be torn away from home. So, your tool for the leak of expectations is to get to know the *Mighty God* and *Everlasting Father* and seek His face for the truth of every situation. God is ready to turn every disappointment into a blessing in disguise.

The Leakage Issue of Relationships

Another one of the problems with the leak in our shower is that the floor is angled in the wrong direction in certain places. This makes the water flow towards the cracks in the grout leading to increased leakage. Similarly, if we are around those who make us flow, by their attitudes and actions away from Jesus' attitudes and actions, our soul will develop serious leaks of the Holy Spirit's power. An important question to ask yourself is, are you moving toward the influences of this world or the influence of Jesus? David Jeremiah reminds us that "inappropriate friendships and relationships can lead us away from God (Deuteronomy 13:6–

9), impact our character and behavior (Proverbs 22:24-25), and cause us to become an enemy of God (James 4:4)."[cxlvi]

Who we hang around matters. As we let ourselves get influenced by those who live by worldly wisdom, the wisdom of God will leak away. Soon we are drained of the sustaining power of God's will and ways. 1 Corinthian 3:19 declares that "For the wisdom of this world is foolishness in God's sight." Foolish choices lead to a foolish soul, and a foolish soul is not a safe place to live. Influence needs to come from Jesus for others. If it goes the other direction, others to our soul towards Jesus He will have to resist. Jesus will never be influenced by anyone but His Father in heaven. To live an abundant life, we must only be influenced by the same source. If someone is being influenced by Jesus, they are someone we can safely be with. When they are not being influenced by Jesus, we must be Jesus's influencer in that relationship. To maintain the home of your soul, we need a tool that will help us flow towards Jesus and away from the foolishness of man, even our own foolishness.

The tool I have found that keeps me away from the flow of the world is what is referred to as the spiritual discipline of formational Bible reading. M. Robert Mulholland Jr. wrote in his book *Invitation to a Journey* that "the classical spiritual discipline of spiritual reading brings us into conflict with the informational priorities of our culture." [cxlvii] Our culture is all about getting information. Thus, it has been called the Information Age. However, when the Bible is read simply for information, transformation seldom happens. As we read God's word, we must let it form us, not try to form it to what we want it to say. As we read to be formed by it, we flow towards the message of Jesus, and He leads us home. We must learn never to read the Bible to get to know the Bible. We must read it to get to know Jesus. Then and only then will the leaks of the influence of the world lose its slant in our lives.

My favorite spiritual discipline when it comes to reading the Bible to get to know Jesus is called Lectio Divina. "Lectio is a posture of approach and a means of encounter with the text that enables the text to become a means of encounter with God,"[cxlviii] says Mulholland. In Lectio Divina, choose a short passage of scripture and then sit in silence, shifting your thoughts toward the voice of the Holy Spirit. Next, you simply read it out loud, like taking a bite of food. When you are done, you go back and read it again, but this time, you chew on it by looking up terms you may not understand and finding out the context of when it was written. Remember, you are seeking to hear what God may be saying, not what we want it to say. Again, when you are done, you read it a third time as a response to God's heart. Let your feelings be affected by it. Last, you read it a final time, surrendering to God's will and the ways the passage has shown you. As you end this time, make a commitment to live out what the Holy Spirit revealed to you. As Jesus' wisdom starts to flow into you, then you won't be as drawn to flow in the wrong direction others are taking.

The Leakage Issue of Busyness

When it comes to maintaining a home, problems put off or ignored will soon make themselves very evident. The previous owners of our house did an amazing job of remodeling it. Over a couple of years, they worked very hard to put incredible details everywhere. Details I am reveling in as I write. They were so busy getting the upstairs done they were too busy to do anything else before they decided to move. As we moved in, we needed to remember that it was still an old house in some places. The basement had not been redone and still sat in the early 1970s. The furnace and air conditioner had not been upgraded because they simply had not gotten to it. This became the source of our next water leakage issue. A malfunctioning air conditioner was freezing up, and every time it was not in use, it would thaw, and water would leak out all over the basement floor.

Busyness can also lead to a leakage issue in our souls. If we are too busy to spend time with Jesus, His Holy Spirit's power will leak. Peter Scazzero writes that "many of us are eager to develop our relationship with God. The problem, however, is that we can't seem to stop long enough to be with Him."[cxlix] The other problem is that we have bought into the lie that if you are not busy doing godly activities, you are a lazy Christian. The truth is that we cannot do any activity for Jesus unless we spend the time to get empowered to do them His way. I heard a story about Heidi Baker where she says she spends most of the morning alone with Jesus. When asked how she could do that and maintain her impressive ministry, she replied that it was the only way she could. Time with Jesus gives us all we need to serve others with Him effectively. Remember, without him, we can't transform anything. When I show up, I don't have much, but when Jesus shows up, he brings the kingdom of God. Therefore, everything is possible. We must not neglect the rhythm of spending time daily getting settled at home with Jesus before all else. Then you carry the kingdom wherever you go.

It was David Jeremiah that taught me that "spiritual growth and power take time and effort. Yes, the Holy Spirit does the changing in us. But we make ourselves available to Him through the spiritual disciplines of prayer, Bible study, worship, service, fellowship, solitude, meditating on Scripture, and others. The psalmist wrote, "Your word I have hidden in my heart that I might not sin against You" (Psalm 119:11). But the Word doesn't get into our life by osmosis. It gets there when we take time to study it, listen to it preached and taught, and discuss it with others."[cl] Even Jesus, while on this earth, purposely spent time with His Father to be refreshed with the wisdom and renewal only God provides. If Jesus, in His humanness, needed to prioritize time with God, I am sure that we must make it a priority to do the same.

The tool to fix the issue of busyness is to commit to practice daily the presence of Jesus, for he is the source of living water that drives all we are and do. Brother Lawrence, the author of *The Practice of the Presence of God,* wrote that "when outward business diverted him a little from the thought of God, a fresh remembrance coming from God invested in his soul, and so inflamed and transported him that it was difficult to contain himself,"[cli] When I spend time with Jesus, I too can't contain all He is and overflow with joy, peace, and wisdom that can only come from the Creator of Heaven and Earth. I become the vessel that reveals His glory. That is the goal of my life. Is it yours? Then join me in keeping the leakage issues of a busy life to take time to stop and make time for Jesus.

The Leakage issue of Storms

Even when everything in the home is working just fine, something on the outside can result in leaks too. Last month we had what the weather people call a "derecho,"[clii] which is a thunderstorm with straight-line winds. During the storm, the rain looked like it was horizontal instead of vertical. The rain came so hard that it started leaking into our window sills and running down the walls. As I put towels down to handle that, I went to our hallway and stepped in a puddle forming under the light. As I looked up, drop by drop, water was flowing out of each of the screws keeping the light in place. I put my head back and closed my eyes with the disgust of realizing I had to deal with some more leakage issues the storm had caused.

    The fact is, storms happen; physically and spiritually. All of them are out of our control, but we still have to deal with the consequences of them. Ice storms, tornados, hail, and flooding all bring the fear of destruction with them. When the storm is over, there are usually messes to clean up and repairs to be done. Just as physical storms require cleaning up down tree branches and possibly repairing the shingles on the roof, spiritual storms will wreak havoc on the home of our soul.

    Spiritual storms come with the uncontrollable elements around us. This sin-damaged world brings the storms of unpredictable, traumatic events, the crisis of a cancer diagnosis, the death of loved ones, and even spiritual forces of evil with the goal it is to keep you from being at home with Jesus. Then there are the storms of rejection, anger, and unintentional wounding words that others hurl at us like hail stones. All of these happen from outside of your control and will affect the home you have created with Jesus. Here too, we must be prepared for them as best we can and have some tools for the repairs that may have to be done in our souls.

    One thing I have discovered is that storms stir up our feelings, especially fear and anxiety. Just look at the disciples in the boat in Matthew chapter 8 when the storm suddenly came upon them. Though Jesus was in the boat with them, and that should have saved them from panic. Instead, they called out, "Lord, save us! We're going to drown!" (v. 25). When our negative feelings are allowed to spread, they take over our ability to think and perceive what is true. Soon those feelings affect every area of our lives like a flood that washes away the foundations of homes in its path.

Dallas Willard wrote that "much of the great power of feelings over life derives not just from the fact that they *touch* us, *move* us, but from the fact that they creep over into other areas of our life; they pervade, they change the overall tone of our life and our world."[cliii] The good news is that feelings can be contained and reasoned with by reality, and asking the question "what is the thoughts behind this feeling?" Making sure we think what is true will help us to take control of the feelings begging to follow them. Willard reminds us that "at all stages of adult life, feelings are among Satan's primary instrument. They are used to devastate the soul in the process of aging, sickness, and death among Christians and non-Christians alike."[cliv]

The good news is that negative feelings don't have to devastate our souls. When we choose to be with Jesus and listen intently to Him, we will be given feelings that help us. Thinking what Jesus thinks gives us love, joy, and peace. Psalm 36:9 says, "in His light we see light." The key to dealing with the storms of our lives is found in Matthew chapter 6. Jesus tells us how to handle feelings of fear and anxiety. He says, "Do not worry about your life" (v. 25). That sure seems easier said than done, right? But Jesus did not stop there. He gave the how-to in verse 33. He says to "seek first His kingdom and His righteousness" In other words, Jesus is saying He has tomorrow all cared for, but you need to take control of your negative feelings by seeking what He says, His will, and His ways.

So, what does that practically look like? Well, like Dallas Willard suggests, we "give [our feelings] up to God… recognize the reality of our feelings and agree with the Lord to abandon those that are destructive and that lead us to do or being what we know is wrong." [clv] We can do this by journaling our feelings like a prayer to Jesus. Ask Jesus to reveal any past events or images that may have been the basis for those destructive feelings, and ask Him to reveal the truth of His love that surrounded you there. Getting the feelings out of our heads and onto paper helps us see them from a new perspective. Our goal is to replace destructive feelings with love, joy, and peace.

Some other suggestions come from Dr. Rob Reimer in his book *Calm in the Storm*. He says to start by taking "responsible action… do what we can do"[clvi] Fear can be paralyzing, and we must purposely choose to step out in intentional, obedient faith. Reimer also suggests that we make sure we are holding on to God's love, keeping an eternal perspective, clinging to the promises of God, turning from self-focus towards Jesus' focus, and giving thanks. His book gives more details, and I highly recommend reading it. I would add to take time to breathe. Breathe in for a count of four, hold for a count of four, and breathe out for a count of four. This gives your mind and body time to relax and stop the panic. Practice the Jesus prayer during this breathing technique. As you breathe in, say, "Lord, Jesus, Son of God" as you hold your breath, remember who Jesus is. Then, as you breathe, simply say, "have mercy on me." Repeat until peace comes to rule the situation.

Every storm gives us the opportunity to be drawn to Jesus or away from Him. If we go away, we become homeless, both emotionally and spiritually. We do have the choice to draw closer to Him and let Jesus fix the destruction that happens in this life. It is in the hardship of life that I have learned the most about how much Jesus loves me. I remember laying on the floor of my bedroom, too devastated to allow myself to lay on the soft bed. I had just learned of my first husband's infidelity and the reality of what that could mean.

Face down on the floor, I chose to cry out to Jesus, and out of the depths of my soul, a song emerged. "My Jesus, I love thee, I know thou art mine; for thee all the follies of sin I resign; my gracious Redeemer, my Savior art thou; if ever I loved thee, my Jesus tis now."[clvii] This song, written 100 years before I was born and not sung since I was a teen, emerged as truth from the One I chose to lean on at that moment. God's love, truth, and faithfulness came when I needed it most. James 4:8 declares that "come near to God, and He will come near to you." The disciples in the Matthew story did that as they ran to Jesus, who was so unworried he could sleep in the storm. They drew near to Jesus, and Jesus calmed the storm. In calming it, he reminded them that having faith in Jesus in the depths of our soul will always get us to where Jesus wants us to be, on the other side with Him.

A Maintained Home is a Sweet Home

Home sweet home is what we hope for. I have a sign by my door that says, "Welcome to our Coffee Sippen' Jesus Lovin' Home Sweet Home." I have realized after all the homes

I have lived in that only a Jesus-lovin home can be truly sweet. The famous old hymn *Tis So Sweet to Trust in Jesus* says it all. "Just to take Him at His Word; Just to rest upon His promise, just to know, "Thus says the Lord!"[clviii] In other words, believe the truth of what God says about you, rest in His love for you and the promise that His love is unconditional, and then know what God says He does. He is trustworthy. When Jesus dwells in your soul through the Holy Spirit, it will be a very sweet place.

Let me go back for a moment to that first house I was describing in chapter one. The dream house where I lived for the hardest three months of my life. The atmosphere was strained with anger, fear, and desperation, that is, except for one room. My bedroom was a place I sought the Lord on those hard nights. I prayed, worshiped, and sought the scriptures for something to help me make it one more day. That room was where Jesus came and ministered to me as my comforter and friend. This made that bedroom different, and the proof came when my parents visited, bringing along one of the foster children living with them.

She had come from a house of chaos and no boundaries. She felt safest in a playpen and had an extra need to feel safe. When my parents entered that house, she started crying immediately. Nothing would comfort her, which was unusual because my parents were amazing at making kids feel safe. We were at a loss for what to do, and so my mom was going to lay down with her. As my mom stepped through my bedroom door, the little girl calmed down instantly. It was kind of weird, so mom walked out, and the crying started again. Back into the bedroom, and calm came. It dawned on me that I could be because I had invited Jesus into that room above all the others and that the atmosphere of His presence brought everything that child needed to feel secure. Where Jesus is invited in acceptance, significance, and security dwell. It is a sweet, lovely place that our souls, like this child, cried out for. Your soul cries for that place too.

Psalm 84: 1-2 says, "How lovely is your dwelling place, O LORD of hosts! My soul longs, yes, faints for the courts of the LORD; my heart and flesh sing for joy to the living God." The place where Jesus our Lord dwells is so sweet our souls long for it like nothing else. Jesus wants to make His home in your soul today. Jesus is knocking on the door (Revelation 3:20) with a longing to bring you everything you need for your life and the power to live like Him (2 Peter 1:3). You have a choice to remain the way you are, homeless emotionally and spiritually or find the place your soul belongs. Your soul belongs with Jesus forever, starting today. Jesus is your forever home, and it can start now before you get to heaven. Everything else you try to fill your soul with only leads to homelessness and hopelessness.

So, it's up to you. As God put it so well in Deuteronomy 30:19, "Today I have given you the choice between life and death, between blessings and curses. Now I call on heaven and earth to witness the choice you make. Oh, that you would choose life, so that you and your descendants might live!"

I have chosen life with Jesus as the home for my soul. I will do the work it takes to maintain it. Won't you join me in doing the same? You can find the place your soul belongs and together, we can help others discover the place their soul belongs; that is with Christ Jesus our all in all.

References

Books Used and Recommended

Anderson, N. T. (2014). *Who I am in christ*. Bethany House Publishers.

Cook, A. K., & Miller, K. (2018). *Boundaries for your soul: How to turn your overwhelming thoughts and feelings into your greatest allies*. Nelson Books.

DeMoss, N. L. (2022). *Lies women believe: And the truth that sets them free*. MOODY PRESS.

Ehman, K. (2016). *Listen, love, repeat: Other-centered living in a self-centered world*. Zondervan.

Hartley, F. (2013). *God on fire*. Clc Publications.

Hartley, F. A., & Gesswein, A. R. (2003). *Everything by prayer: Armin Gesswein's keys to spirit-filled living*. Christian Publications.

Jethani, S. (2011). *With: Reimagining the way you relate to god*. Thomas Nelson.

Lawrence, B (2009). *The practice of the presence of god: Conversations and Letters of brother Lawrence*. Oneworld.

Mulholland, M. R., & Barton, R. R. (2016). *Invitation to a journey: A road map for spiritual formation*. InterVarsity Press.

Murray, A. (2021). *Absolute surrender*. Antiquarius.

Reese, A., Anderson, N., & Barnett, J. (2008). *Freedom tools: For overcoming life's tough problems*. Chosen Books.

Regier, J. (1999). *Biblical concepts counseling workbook: Identifying and resolving personal and marital problems biblically*. Biblical Concepts in Counseling.

Reimer, R (2022). *Calm in the Storm*. Biblica.

Reimer, R. (2015). *River dwellers: Living in the fullness of the spirit*. Carpenters Son Pub.

Reimer, R. (2016). *Soul care 7 transformational principles for a healthy soul*. Carpenters Son Pub.

Scazzero, P. (2019). *Emotionally healthy spirituality*. Duranno Press.

Speake, W. (2019). *The 40-day sugar fast: Where Physical Detox meets Spiritual transformation*. Baker Books.

TerKeurst, L. (2018). *It's not supposed to be this way: Finding unexpected strength when disappointments leave you shattered*. Nelson Books, an imprint of Thomas Nelson.

Willard, D. (2021). *Renovation of the heart: Putting on the character of christ*. NavPress.

Names of Jesus from A to Z

A

Advocate - 1 John 2:1
Alive for Evermore - Revelation 1:18
All-Knowing - Psalm 139:1-6
All, and in All - Colossians 3:11
Almighty - Revelation 1:8
Alpha and Omega - Revelation 1:8
Altar - Hebrews 13:10
Altogether Lovely - Song of Solomon 5:16
Amen - Revelation 3:14
Ancient of Days - Daniel 7:13 & Daniel 7:22
Anointed One - 1 Samuel 2:35
Author of Eternal Salvation - Hebrews 5:9
Author of our Faith - Hebrews 12:2

B

Balm of Gilead - Jeremiah 8:22
Banner over us - Ps 60:4 S of Sol 2:4
Bearer of Sin - Hebrews 9:28
Before All Things - Colossians 1:17
Beginning and Ending - Revelation 1:8
Bishop of our Souls - 1 Peter 2:25
Blessed and Only Potentate - 1 Timothy 6:15
Blessed Hope - Titus 2:13
Bread of Life, my manna - John 6:35
Bridegroom - John 3:29
Bright and Morning Star - Revelation 22:16
Brightness of His Glory - Hebrews 1:3
Buckler - Psalms 18:30

C

Captain - Joshua 5:14-15 - Hebrews 2:10
Changeless One - Malachi 3:6, Hebrews 13:8
Chief Among 10,000 - S. of Solomon 5:10
Chosen of God - 1 Peter 2:4
Christ - Matthew 1:16 - 1 John 5:1
Comforter - John 14:16-18
Consolation of Israel - Luke 2:25
Counselor - Isaiah 9:6
Creator - Romans 1:25 - Isaiah 40:28
Crown of Glory - Isaiah 28:5

D

Daystar to Arise - 2 Peter 1:19
Defense - Psalms 94:22
Deliverer - Psalms 40:17
Desire of all Nations - Haggai 2:7
Despised and rejected - Ps 22:6, Is 53:3
Diadem of Beauty - Isaiah 28:5
Door of the Sheep - John 10:7
Dwelling Place - Psalms 90:1

E

Emmanuel - Matthew 1:23
End of the Law - Romans 10:4
Ensign of the People - Isaiah 11:10
Equal with God - Philippians 2:6
Eternal God - Deuteronomy 33:27
Eternal Life - 1 John 1:2
Everlasting Father - Isaiah 9:6

F

Faithful and True - Rev 19:11 - Rev 3:14
Finisher of the Faith - Hebrews 12:2
First Begotten - Hebrews 1:6 - Romans 8:29
Fortress - Psalms 18:2
Foundation Which is Laid - 1 Cor.3:11
Fountain of Living Waters – Jer. 17:13 Ps 36:9
Friend of Publicans and Sinners - Luke 7:34
Friend Sticks Closer than a brother - Prov 18:24

G

Gift of God - John 4:10
Glory, my and lifter of my head - Psalms 3:3
God Who Avenges Me - Psalms 18:47
God Blessed Forever - Romans 9:5
God Who Forgives - Psalms 99:8
God of My Life - Psalms 42:8
God in the Midst of Her - Psalms 46:5
God manifest in the flesh - 1 Timothy 3:16
God of My Righteousness - Psalms 4:1
God of My Salvation - Psalms 18:46
God of My Strength - Psalms 43:2
God With Us - Matthew 1:23
Good Shepherd - John 10:11
Gracious - Ex 33:19, Rom 16:24, Rev. 22:21
Great God - Titus 2:13
Great Shepherd of the Sheep - Hebrews 13:20
Guide Even Unto Death - Psalms 48:14

H

Harmless - Hebrews 7:26
Head of all Principality & Power - Col 2:10
Heir of All Things - Hebrews 1:2
Helper - Hebrews 13:6
Hiding Place - Psalms 32:7
High Priest Forever - Hebrews 6:20
High Tower - Psalms 18:2
Holy One Of Israel - Psalms 89:18
Horn of Salvation - Luke 1:69
Husband - Revelation 21:2

I

I Am - John 18:6
Image of the Invisible God - Colossians 1:15
Immanuel - Isaiah 7:14
Inhabiter of Eternity - Isaiah 57:15
Inhabiter of Praises - Psalms 22:3

Intercessor - Isaiah 53:12 & Romans 8:34

J

Jehovah Jireh - Provider - I Jn 4:9, Philip 4:19
Jehovah Nissi - Banner - I Chronicles 29:11-13
Jehovah Shalom - Peace - Is 9:6, Rom 8:31-35
Jehovah Tsidkenu - Righteousness - I Cor 1:30
Jehovah Shammah - Present - Hebrews 13:5
Jehovah M'Kaddesh - Sanctifier - I Cor 1:30
Jehovah Rophe - Healer - Isaiah 53:4,5
Jehovah Rohi - Shepherd - Psalm 23
Jesus - Matthew 1:21
Jesus Christ Our Lord - Romans 7:25
Judge of All - Genesis 18:25 - Acts 10:42
Just One - Acts 7:52

K

Keeper - Psalms 121:5
King Eternal - 1 Timothy 1:17
King Immortal - 1 Timothy 1:17
King Invisible - 1 Timothy 1:17
King of Glory - Psalms 24:7-8
King of Heaven - Daniel 4:37
King of Kings - Revelation 19:16
King of Peace - Hebrews 7:2
King of Righteousness - Hebrews 7:2
King of Saints - Revelation 15:3

L

Lamb of God - John 1:29 - Rev 17:14
Lamb Slain - Rev 13:8 - Rev 5:12 - Rev 7:17
Last Adam - 1 Cor.15:45
Lawgiver - James 4:12
Life - John 14:6
Lifter of Mine Head - Psalms 3:3
Light - John 1:7
Light of the World - John 8:12
Lily of the Valleys - Song of Solomon 2:1
Lion of the Tribe of Judah - Revelation 5:5
Living Bread - John 6:51
Lord and My God - John 20:28
Lord and Savior - 2 Peter 1:11
Lord of the Dead and the Living - Rom 14:9
Lord God Almighty - Revelation 16:7
Lord God Omnipotent - Revelation 19:6
Lord Jesus Christ - James 2:1
Lord of Glory - 1 Cor.2:8
Lord of the Harvest - Matthew 9:38
Lord of Lords - 1 Timothy 6:15

M

Maker - Psalms 95:6
Man of Sorrows - Isaiah 53:3
Master - Matthew 23:10
Mediator - 1 Timothy 2:5
Merciful - Heb 2:17
Messiah the Prince - Daniel 9:25
Mighty God - Isaiah 9:6
Morning Star - Revelation 2:28

N

Name Above Every Name - Philippians 2:9
Nazarene - Matthew 2:23

O

Omega - Revelation 22:13
Omnipotent - Revelation 19:6
Only Begotten Son - John 3:16
Only Potentate - 1 Timothy 6:15
Only Wise God - 1 Timothy 1:17

P

Passover, my - 1 Cor.5:7
Pavilion - Psalms 31:20
Peace, our - Ephesians 2:14
Physician, great - Luke 4:23
Portion of Mine Inheritance - Psalms 16:5
Potter - Jeremiah 18:6
Power of God - 1 Cor.1:24
Preeminent one - Colossians 1:18
Pearl of Price - Matt 13:46, 1 Cor.6:20
Prince of Peace - Isaiah 9:6
Propitiation for Our Sins - 1 John 2:2

Q

Quick Understanding - Isaiah 11:3
Quickening Spirit - 1 Cor.15:45

R

Rabbi - John 3:2
Ransom for Many - Matthew 20:28
Redeemer - Job 19:25 - 1 Cor.1:30
Refiner - Malachi 3:2
Refuge in Trouble - Ps 46:1, Ps 9:9
Refuge from the Storm - Is 25:4
Resting Place - Jeremiah 50:6
Resurrection and the Life - John 11:25
Reward of the Righteous - Psalms 58:11
Righteous Judge - 2 Timothy 4:8
Righteousness, my - 1 Cor.1:30 - Rom 10:3
Rock that is Higher than I - Psalms 61:2
Rock of My Refuge - Psalms 94:22
Rock of Our Salvation - Psalms 95:1
Root and Offspring of David - Revelation 22:16
Rose of Sharon – Song of Solomon 2:1

S

Sacrifice for Sins - Hebrews 10:12
Salvation, my - Psalms 27:1
Same Yesterday, Today, Forever - Heb 13:8
Savior of the Body - Ephesians 5:23
Savior of the World - John 4:42
Scapegoat - Leviticus 16:8 & John 11:49-52
Scepter of Israel - Numbers 24:17
Sent One - John 9:4
Separate from Sinners - Hebrews 7:26
Serpent in the Wilderness - John 3:14
Shadow of the Almighty - Psalms 91:1

Shadow of a Great Rock - Isaiah 32:2
Shelter - Psalms 61:3
Shepherd, my - Psalms 23:1
Shield - Psalms 84:9
Sin, for us - 2 Cor.5:21
Son of God - John 1:49
Son of Man - John 1:51
Song, my - Isaiah 12:2
Spiritual Rock - 1 Cor.10:4
Star out of Jacob - Numbers 24:17
Stone the Builders Rejected - Matthew 21:42
Strength of My Life - Psalms 27:1
Stronghold in the Day of Trouble - Nahum 1:7
Strong Tower - Proverbs 18:10
Stronger than the enemy - Luke 11:22
Sun of Righteousness - Malachi 4:2

T

Tabernacle of God - Revelation 21:3
Tender Plant - Isaiah 53:2
Testator - Hebrews 9:16
Treasure - 2 Cor.4:7
True Bread from Heaven - John 6:32
True Light - John 1:9
True Vine - John 15:1
Truth - John 14:6

U

Undefiled - Hebrews 7:26
Unspeakable Gift - 2 Cor.9:15
Upholder of All things - Hebrews 1:3
Upright - Psalms 92:15

V

Very God of Peace - 1 Thessalonians 5:23
Very Present Help in Trouble - Psalms 46:1
Victory - 1 Cor.15:54
Vine - John 15:5
Voice - Revelation 1:12

W

Way - John 14:6
Well of Living Waters - John 4:14
Wisdom of God - 1 Cor.1:24
Wise Master Builder - 1 Cor.3:10
Witness of God - 1 John 5:9
Wonderful - Isaiah 9:6
Word - John 1:1 - Revelation 19:13
Worthy - Revelation 4:11
Worthy Name - James 2:7

X

Exceeding Great Reward - Genesis 15:1
Excellency - Job 13:11
Excellency of Our God - Isaiah 35:2
Excellent - Psalms 8:1
Express Image of His Person - Hebrews 1:3

Y

Young Child - Matthew 2:11
Yes and Amen - 2 Cor 1:20

Z

Zeal of the Lord of Hosts - Isaiah 37:32
Zeal of your House - John 2:17

Notes

[i] https://www.merriam-webster.com/dictionary/home, n.d.
[ii] https://www.goodreads.com/quotes/400883-the-ache-for-home-lives-in-all-of-us-the
[iii] https://www.gotquestions.org/soul-care.html
[iv] Colossians 1:27 NIV
[v] Luke 22:54-62
[vi] Acts 2:1-4
[vii] Luke 22:57
[viii] Acts 5:15
[ix] Joshua 1:9, Matthew 28:20, Psalms 139:7-8
[x] God on Fire by Fred A Hartley III/chapter 1 page 29
[xi] https://www.merriam-webster.com/dictionary/manifest
[xii] Genesis 3:8
[xiii] Exodus 3:1-17
[xiv] Daniel 5:5
[xv] John 16:7 CEV
[xvi] Acts 16:7
[xvii] https://billygraham.org/devotion/our-eternal-home/
[xviii] River Dwellers by Dr. Rob Reimer
[xix] https://www.britannica.com/topic/cultivation
[xx] Luke 8:8
[xxi] Luke 8:14b
[xxii] https://endhomelessness.org/homelessness-in-america/homelessness-statistics/state-of-homelessness-report/
[xxiii] https://www.ronitbaras.com/emotional-intelligence/personal-development/six-human-needs-certainty/
[xxiv] Exodus 14-24
[xxv] Ephesians 1:14
[xxvi] https://www.hymnal.net/en/hymn/h/582
[xxvii] 2 Peter 1:3
[xxviii] Genesis 2:25
[xxix] Revelation 12:1-12
[xxx] 2 Corinthians 4:4
[xxxi] Genesis 3:1-7
[xxxii] Genesis 3:23
[xxxiii] Genesis 2:9
[xxxiv] https://www.npr.org/2009/07/27/111091624/homeless-man-leaves-behind-surprise-4-million
[xxxv] John 10:10
[xxxvi] Luke 15:11-32
[xxxvii] Psalm 68:19
[xxxviii] Emotionally Healthy Spirituality by Peter Scazzero; Chapter 1, page 12

[xxxix] Romans 6:11
[xl] John 10:10
[xli] https://www.psychologytoday.com/us/blog/the-power-prime/201908/perception-is-not-reality
[xlii] https://www.parents.com/baby/development/social/birth-order-and-personality/
[xliii] Alliman M.A, Roger; Surley M.A., Rick, Counseling Theory and the Scriptures. Page 9
[xliv] https://thecusp.com.au/does-comparing-yourself-to-your-sibling-affect-who-you-are/9458
[xlv] http://www.sylviarimm.com/article_sibcomp.html
[xlvi] https://www.charismanews.com/opinion/the-pulse/53573-15-ways-hurting-people-hurt-people
[xlvii] Soul Care by Rob Reimer page 100
[xlviii] https://www.scientificamerican.com/article/harsh-parents-raise-bullies-so-do-permissive-ones/
[xlix] https://www.psychologytoday.com/us/blog/the-couch/201801/betrayed-your-best-friend-6-ways-heal-your-heart
[l] Emotionally Healthy Spirituality by Peter Scazzero; Chapter 1, page 19
[li] https://www.goodreads.com/quotes/50997-the-most-terrible-poverty-is-loneliness-and-the-feeling-of
[lii] http://www.sermonindex.net/modules/newbb/viewtopic.php?topic_id=34520&forum=35
[liii] Deuteronomy 31:6
[liv] https://www.hgtv.com/shows/fixer-upper/episodes/first-time-buyers-take-a-chance-on-a-vintage-fixer-upper
[lv] Isaiah 28:16
[lvi] Matthew 7:26
[lvii] https://www.merriam-webster.com/dictionary/identity
[lviii] Genesis 1:27
[lix] https://exploringyourmind.com/energy-others-give-off-affects-feel/
[lx] Lies Women Believe and the Truth That Sets Them Free by Nancy Leigh DeMoss, Chapter 1 page 32
[lxi] 2 Corinthians 11:14
[lxii] Soul Care by Rob Reimer page 52-58
[lxiii] Soul Care by Rob Reimer page 56
[lxiv] John 15:16
[lxv] 1 Corinthians 1:2; Ephesians 1:1; Philippians 1:1; Colossians 1:2
[lxvi] Romans 8:17
[lxvii] John 15:15
[lxviii] Who I am in Christ: A Devotional, Neil T. Anderson 2001
[lxix] Soul Care by Rob Reimer page 125
[lxx] https://greatergood.berkeley.edu/topic/forgiveness/definition
[lxxi] https://www.mayoclinic.org/healthy-lifestyle/adult-health/in-depth/forgiveness/art-20047692

[lxxii] Biblical Concepts Counseling Workbook by John Regier page 29
[lxxiii] https://en.wikipedia.org/wiki/Maslow%27s_hierarchy_of_needs#/media/File:MaslowsHierarchyOfNeeds.svg
[lxxiv] http://psychclassics.yorku.ca/Maslow/motivation.htm
[lxxv] https://www.informationng.com/2013/08/end-of-the-world-american-family-build-doomsday-castle-to-survive-the-apocalypse.html
[lxxvi] https://www.oddee.com/item_98962.aspx
[lxxvii] https://www.bing.com/search?pc=COS2&ptag=D112618-N0610A21ABFDD9D88F4162B1F&conlogo=CT3332016&q=define+trust&form=CONBDF
[lxxviii] Wendy Speaks; The 40-day Sugar Fast; Day 33
[lxxix] Proverbs 14:1
[lxxx] Jeremiah 31:4
[lxxxi] https://resurrectedliving.wordpress.com/2013/10/03/dietrich-bonhoeffer-on-overcoming-fear/
[lxxxii] Soul Care by Rob Reimer page 187
[lxxxiii] John 8:32
[lxxxiv] John 8:17
[lxxxv] Twitter @gemsgirlsclubs
[lxxxvi] https://www.biblestudytools.com/lexicons/greek/nas/sozo.html
[lxxxvii] Freedom Tools by Andy Reese Chapter 1 page 25
[lxxxviii] John 16:13
[lxxxix] https://resurrectedliving.wordpress.com/2013/10/03/dietrich-bonhoeffer-on-overcoming-fear/
[xc] Matthew 28:20
[xci] Hebrews 13:5
[xcii] With, Reimagining the Way You Relate to God by Skye Jethani, Chapter 6 pages 109-110
[xciii] John 20:26
[xciv] Fred A. Hartley III, "Lord, As Families, Teach Us to Pray!" College of Prayer Year Two Notebook, Second Edition
[xcv] https://www.goodreads.com/work/quotes/13462590-one-thousand-gifts
[xcvi] https://quoteinvestigator.com/2012/05/06/other-plans/
[xcvii] 2 Corinthians 10:3-4
[xcviii] I Surrender All; SONG WRITER: Judson VanDeVenter
[xcix] Luke 22:42
[c] Andrew Murray, Absolute Surrender
[ci] Andrew Murray, Absolute Surrender
[cii] https://www.goodreads.com/quotes/tag/surrender
[ciii] https://www.thefreedictionary.com/living-room
[civ] With, Reimagining the Way You Relate to God by Skye Jethani, Chapter 6 pages 115
[cv] https://www.facebook.com/OfficialLysa/posts/10156388576692694

[cvi] Everything by Prayer: Armin Gesswein's Keys to Spirit Filled Living by Fred A Hartley III Chapter 3 verse 52
[cvii] Everything by Prayer: Armin Gesswein's Keys to Spirit Filled Living by Fred A Hartley III Chapter 3 verse 53
[cviii] https://www.collegeofprayer.org
[cix] River Dwellers, Living in the Fullness of the Spirit by Dr. Rob Reimer Chapter 3 page 106
[cx] John 10:27
[cxi] Luke 22:42
[cxii] https://orthodoxprayer.org/Jesus%20Prayer.html
[cxiii] John 1:1
[cxiv] River Dwellers, Living in the Fullness of the Spirit by Dr. Rob Reimer Chapter 3
[cxv] Matthew 4:1-11
[cxvi] John 10:10
[cxvii] Soul Care by Rob Reimer, page 7
[cxviii] Soul Care by Rob Reimer, page 44
[cxix] https://www.thegospelcoalition.org/article/repentance-vs-defensiveness/
[cxx] https://www.mentalhelp.net/advice/what-is-the-true-meaning-of-being-defensive/
[cxxi] https://www.thegospelcoalition.org/article/repentance-vs-defensiveness/
[cxxii] https://www.biblestudytools.com/dictionary/peace/
[cxxiii] Cook & Miller, Boundaries for Your Soul, p. 199-200
[cxxiv] https://www.focusonthefamily.com/marriage/keeping-the-peace-at-any-price/
[cxxv] Luke 9:42
[cxxvi] John 11:35
[cxxvii] Matthew 14:13-14
[cxxviii] Matthew 6:34
[cxxix] Mark 10:21
[cxxx] Karen Ehman; Listen, Love, Repeat: Other centered living in a self-centered world. Chapter 3
[cxxxi] Karen Ehman; Listen, Love, Repeat: Other centered living in a self-centered world. Chapter 5
[cxxxii] Luke 8:43-48
[cxxxiii] Romans 12:12
[cxxxiv] Mark 9:7
[cxxxv] Revelation 2:7; 2:11; 2:17; 2:29; 3:6; 3:13; 3:22
[cxxxvi] http://www.differencebetween.net/science/nature/difference-between-listening-and-hearing/
[cxxxvii] https://www.youtube.com/watch?v=J5W36VWNd9E
[cxxxviii] Karen Ehman; Listen, Love, Repeat: Other centered living in a self-centered world. Chapter 9
[cxxxix] Who I Am in Christ; A Devotional. Neil Anderson p. 22

[cxl] Mark 4:9
[cxli] Who I Am in Christ; A Devotional. Neil Anderson p. 23
[cxlii] https://www.simplypsychology.org/maslow.html
[cxliii] Who I Am in Christ; A Devotional. Neil Anderson p. 105
[cxliv] https://www.davidjeremiah.org/makingsense/failures/feeling-drained-you-might-have-one-of-those-four-spiritual-leaks?devdate=2021-03-23
[cxlv] Lysa TerKeurst, It's Not Supposed to Be This Way: Finding Unexpected Strength When Disappointments Leave You Shattered

[cxlvi] https://www.davidjeremiah.org/makingsense/failures/feeling-drained-you-might-have-one-of-those-four-spiritual-leaks?devdate=2021-03-23
[cxlvii] M. Robert Mulholland Jr. Invitation to a Journey: A Road Map for Spiritual Formation p. 127
[cxlviii] M. Robert Mulholland Jr. Invitation to a Journey: A Road Map for Spiritual Formation p. 129
[cxlix] Emotionally Healthy Spirituality, Workbook by Peter and Geri Scazzero p.81
[cl] https://www.davidjeremiah.org/makingsense/failures/feeling-drained-you-might-have-one-of-those-four-spiritual-leaks?devdate=2021-03-23
[cli] The Practice of the Presence of God, Brother Lawrence p.13
[clii] https://www.foxweather.com/learn/what-is-a-derecho
[cliii] Renovation of the Heart, Dallas Willard p. 124
[cliv] Renovation of the Heart, Dallas Willard p. 139
[clv] Renovation of the Heart, Dallas Willard p. 137
[clvi] Calm in the Strom, Rob Reimer p. 36
[clvii] My Jesus, I Love Thee; William Featherston, 1862
[clviii] Tis So Sweet to Trust in Jesus; music by William J. Kirkpatrick, lyrics by Louisa M. Stead

www.ingramcontent.com/pod-product-compliance
Lightning Source LLC
Chambersburg PA
CBHW072102050526
44107CB00099B/346